Contents

KU-608-098

Figures, Tables and Boxes

FIGURES

TABLES

BOXES

Acronyms and Abbreviations

AWEA	American Wind Energy Association
BFF	Best Foot Forward
DTI	Department of Trade and Industry
ECU	European Currency Unit
DETR	Department of the Environment, Transport, and the Regions
EEA	European Environmental Agency
EFA	ecological footprint analysis
EPE	environmental performance evaluation
ETSU	Energy Technology Support Unit (DETR, UK)
EU	European Union
FoE	Friends of the Earth
FAO	Food and Agricultural Organization (UN)
GIS	Geographical Information System
GNP	gross national product
GDP	gross domestic product
GPI	genuine progress indicator
ICLEI	International Council for Local Environmental Initiatives
IEA	International Energy Agency
IFPRI	International Food Policy Research Institute
ISEW	Index of Sustainable Economic Welfare
IIED	International Institute for Environment and Development
IPAT	impact = population x affluence x technology
IPCC	Intergovernmental Panel on Climate Change
IUCN	World Conservation Union
LPG	liquified petroleum gas
LCA	life cycle analysis
MIPS	material intensity per unit of service
OECD	Organisation for Economic Cooperation and Development
PIRA	Paper Industry Research Association
PV	photovoltaics
RIVM	National Institute of Public Health and Environment (The Netherlands)
SPI	sustainable process index
TMF	total materials flows
UBP	Union Bancaire Privée

UN	United Nations
UNCED	United Nations Conference on Environment and Development
UNDP	United Nations Development Programme
UNEP	United Nations Environment Programme
UNCTAD	United Nations Conference on Trade and Development
WBCSD	World Business Council on Sustainable Development
WEF	World Economic Forum
WWF	World Wide Fund For Nature
WRI	World Resources Institute

Preface

When *Our Ecological Footprint* was published in early 1996 it struck a chord with many that read it. The book opened the door to an exciting new way of measuring and communicating sustainability using an area-based indicator.

Yet we did not first encounter ecological footprinting on the pages of this excellent book. Instead we learned of the methodology via a second-hand conversation from someone inspired by an early presentation given by Mathis in Oxford.

The few snatched phrases that were related from Mathis' talk set us thinking about the possible applications of the methodology. Somewhat deliberately, we avoided reading Mathis' and Bill Rees' work until we had reached our own conclusions – the result being what we refer to today as the component footprinting methodology.

Inevitably, we were strongly influenced by our collective background in environmental training, business and governmental policy-making, resource analysis, software ergonomics and consumer psychology. Our emphasis and interests remain the development of a generic framework and tool set to inform and influence those involved in sustainable development at all levels.

The growing popularity of ecological footprinting has led to a steady stream of calls, papers and emails to the Best Foot Forward offices. It rapidly became clear to us that very little of the research into the methodology was in an appropriate format for decision-makers and practitioners. Together we set about packaging it into more instructive, bite-sized chunks for non-technical audiences. We took advantage of the increasing availability of computer technology to develop user-friendly computer interfaces to make the application of ecological footprint analysis more natural and transparent.

By the time we caught up with Mathis for a serious chat in early 1998 we were already enjoying some success in the UK with EcoCal, a computer-based footprinting tool aimed at helping households explore their impact on the environment. Mathis convinced us of the need to rationalize the calculations used to derive component footprints and over the next two years he gave generously of both his experience and infectious enthusiasm.

This book largely grew out of several meetings with Mathis and seemingly hundreds of email exchanges. It is but a snapshot of the developments in this field. Applications of the methodology continue at an ever-increasing pace.

We hope that through the pages of this book, and the accompanying website, we can help to focus the broad debate on environmental sustainability and, most importantly, encourage widespread action.

Nicky Chambers
Craig Simmons
Oxford, England
August 2000

As if it were yesterday, I remember the unexpected email that found its way to me in September 1997 as I was cruising through Sweden on a lecture and research trip. Thanks to the magic electronic spider's web that spans the world, Nicky had tracked down my address and told me about their work at Best Foot Forward. And I was moved. She claimed that they had gotten so excited about footprinting that it not only infected their company's name, but had led to the development of a whole line of products to give footprint thinking more traction. I was even more taken by the fact that their entire consultancy was focusing its efforts on sustainability advocacy that was based not on vague, feel-good language but on the recognition that there is only one life-sustaining planet within human reach.

Their focus on solutions is echoed in the communiqué announcing their first software packages in 1997: 'Our aim is to make it easier for companies, public bodies and individuals to measure and understand the magnitude of their impact on the environment and for them to determine what they need to do to act sustainably.'

At this time I was still operating out of Anáhuac University, at the Centre for Sustainability Studies in Xalapa, Mexico, where we had just completed our first detailed footprint study of 52 nations, originally commissioned by the RIO+5 Forum. As this study created a demand that kept me busy on the lecture circuit, it took no more than a few months before I passed through Oxford, where we could meet face to face. During those intense days of meeting and exchanging stories, we felt tickled by the idea of joining forces for a practical, yet engaging, book on footprinting. Craig and Nicky's experience was with user-friendly software design, participation in business initiatives for sustainability, and a long-standing engagement with the sustainability initiatives of local and national governments. These served as great complements to my exposure to academic circles and NGOs on both sides of the Atlantic, as well as my interest in methodological advancements of footprint accounts coupled with the challenge of effectively communicating the realities of global and national overshoot. This book is the result.

Nicky and Craig's work is proof that the footprint has graduated from an obscure academic idea, mainly used to make students sweat at their exams, to a tool with practical, real-world applications. Their work has added weight to the over 4000 websites that discuss the ecological footprint, and to a plethora of government documents and business advertising that refer to the footprint idea. In the early stages, much of my motivation came from demonstrating why the dominant system was socially and ecologically devastating, with no conviction that sustainability could actually be reached. Now, the growing interest in and enthusiasm toward making satisfying lives possible for everyone, whilst living within our planet's ecological means, has taught me that sustainability can actually be won. More and more evidence strengthens my sense that the tide may be turning. Not yet quickly enough. But we know sustainability is possible and achievable. And the strengthening of this possibility is the driver behind today's footprint work.

That's why I am particularly grateful to Nicky and Craig since they operate from the conviction that living in a sustainable world is a valid option. I am proud to count them among my colleagues and thank them warmly for this wonderful collaboration.

Mathis Wackernagel
Oakland, California
August 2000

Acknowledgements

The authors would like to thank the staff at Best Foot Forward, Redefining Progress and The Centre for Sustainability Studies for their support during the gestation of this book. In particular we would like to single out Kevin Lewis and P V Vernon in Oxford, Diana Deumling in Oakland, and Alejandro Callejas Linares, María Antonieta Vásquez Sánchez and Ina Susana López Falfán in Xalapa, Mexico, for their invaluable contributions. Thanks are also due to Elizabeth J de Mello for her ongoing support.

Our enthusiasm for taking the environmental sustainability message to a wider audience has thankfully been shared by many friends and colleagues. Their comments, suggestions and ideas have woven their way into the finished text. A special mention to Duncan McLaren and Oliver Tickell who reviewed early drafts, and Alex Long and Gary Goodman who gave advice on structuring sections of this book. They all helped us steer a steadier course. We are also indebted to Bill Rees, whose thinking has touched us all. As a human ecologist, and co-originator of the ecological footprint concept, his work underpins much of the content.

These acknowledgements would be incomplete without thanking our partners Andy, Elise and Susan who have acted as sounding-boards and unpaid proofreaders throughout.

Introduction

'In our way of life... with every decision we make, we always keep in mind the Seventh Generation of children to come... When we walk upon Mother Earth we always plant our feet carefully, because we know that the faces of future generations are looking up at us from beneath the ground. We never forget them' (Oren Lyons, Faithkeeper, Onondaga Nation, Earth Day 1993 Pledge)

Every organism, be it a bacterium, whale or person, has an impact on the earth. We all rely upon the products and services of nature, both to supply us with raw materials and to assimilate our wastes. The impact we have on our environment is related to the 'quantity' of nature that we use or 'appropriate' to sustain our consumption patterns.

The key question is whether this load exceeds what nature can sustainably support. There is only a finite amount of natural resources in the planet's ecological bank account. If we continually deplete this capital then – eventually – we will have nothing left to draw upon. Instead, we must learn to live within nature's interest, sharing the bounty with the tumultuous diversity of other life on this planet.

In this book, we describe one practical method that allows us to explore and manage our impact on the environment. Using ecological footprint analysis it is possible to estimate the area of land that would be necessary to sustainably support consumption levels.[1]

It is said that every journey starts with a single step. The authors' hope is that this book will encourage you to try out ecological footprinting for yourself and to understand more about your relationship with the natural world.

You have within your power a great gift for future generations, and that is learning to live better on a smaller footprint.

Enjoy life and share in nature's interest.

Nicky Chambers
Craig Simmons[2]
Mathis Wackernagel[3]

NOTES

1   The first comprehensive publication on ecological footprinting is *Our Ecological Footprint: Reducing Human Impact on the Earth*, Mathis Wackernagel and William E Rees, New Society Publishers, Gabriola Island, BC, 1996. It has been translated to various languages including: Italian (through Edizioni Ambiente, Milan), German (through Birkhäuser Verlag, Basel) and French (Ecosocieté, Montreal)

2   Craig and Nicky are co-Founders and Directors of Best Foot Forward Limited, The Future Centre, 115 Magdalen Road, Oxford, OX4 1RQ, UK. Web: www.bestfootforward.com, email: mail@bestfootforward.com

3   Mathis is a Program Director at Redefining Progress, 1904 Franklin Street, 6th Floor, Oakland, CA 94612, USA and Coordinator of the Centre for Sustainability Studies / Centro de Estudios para la Sustentabilidad, Universidad Anáhuac de Xalapa, Xalapa, Ver, Mexico. Web: http://www.rprogress.org, email: wackernagel@rprogress.org

Chapter 1

Redefining Progress

'Progress means getting nearer the place you want to be. And if you take a wrong turning, then to go forward does not get you any nearer. If you are on the wrong road, progress means doing an about face and walking back to the right road, and in that case the man who turns back the soonest is the most progressive man' (C S Lewis in *'Mere Christianity'*)[1]

SUSTAINABLE DEVELOPMENT

What will the world be like in 2050? By that time the human race will have had to face up to many environmental and social barriers to real progress. To take just a few examples:

- How can we feed a global population predicted to be half as big again as at the turn of this century?
- Can we succeed in eliminating poverty and inequality whilst providing an acceptable quality of life for all?
- Will we be able to harness enough energy to power our economies without damaging environmental consequences?
- Can we halt the decline in biodiversity and learn to live in harmony with other species?

These are just some of the big questions that society has only recently begun to address under the umbrella term of 'sustainable development'.

In 1987 the Brundtland report *Our Common Future* popularized the use of this phrase, defining it as, 'meeting the needs of the present without compromising the ability of future generations to meet their own needs'. Former UK Environment Minister John Gummer put it more succinctly when he said that sustainable development amounts to 'not cheating on our children'.

Box 1.1 Some Further Attempts at Defining Sustainable Development

Friends of the Earth: 'Meeting the twin needs of protecting the environment and alleviating poverty'[2]

UK Government: Social progress which recognizes the needs of everyone, effective protection of the environment, prudent use of natural resources, maintenance of high and stable levels of economic growth and employment.[3]

Sir Crispin Tickell: Sustainable Development is 'treating the earth as if we meant to stay'[4]

The Body Shop: 'Sustainability and sustainable development remain elusive concepts. They have variously been referred to as, for instance, "vision expression", "value change", "moral development", "social reorganization", or "transformational process"'.[5]

Steve Goldfinger (on ecological sustainability): 'Turn resources into junk no faster than nature can turn junk back into resources'.[6]

See also Pearce, D, Markandya, A, and Barbier, E, 1989, *Blueprint for a Green Economy*, Earthscan, London.

There are many other equally valid definitions (for examples see Boxes 1.1 and 1.2). Despite the number and variety of definitions, there are certain common principles that have gained widespread acceptance:

- Human quality of life ultimately depends on, amongst other things, a healthy and productive environment to provide both goods and services and a pleasant place to live.
- The needs of the poor must be met, providing at least a basic quality of life for all of the world's population.
- Future generations should have the same opportunity to harness the world's resources as the current generation.

The maintenance of human well-being relies on the provision of goods and services. That is not to say that all things that enrich our lives depend on material consumption, merely that many do. We need energy for heat and mobility, wood for housing, furniture and paper products, fibres for clothing, and food and water to sustain us.

These in turn rely on an intricate web of natural processes to maintain the quality of the air, fertility of the soil, fresh water and more besides. We all depend on nature both to supply us with resources and absorb our waste.

But, to paraphrase the title of Al Gore's book, the earth is in balance.[7] Living beyond our ecological means will surely lead to the degradation of our only home; human well-being will suffer.

Similarly, having insufficient natural resources and living in unsatisfactory and inequitable ways will cause conflict and degrade our social fabric.

To make sustainability happen, we need to balance the basic conflict between the two competing goals of ensuring a quality of life and living within the limits of nature. Humanity must resolve the tension between ultimate ends (a good life for everybody) and ultimate means (the capacity of the biosphere).[8]

In this context, one of the most helpful and practical definitions of sustainable development is 'improving the quality of life while living within the carrying capacity of supporting ecosystems'.[9]

Finding ways to meet this challenge is the focus of this book. Let us start with a closer look at what is meant by sustainability, consumption and quality of life.

SUSTAINABILITY, CONSUMPTION AND QUALITY OF LIFE

The *Collins Dictionary* definition of consume is 'v. to destroy or use up' and consumption 'expenditure on goods and services for final personal use'.

Many aspects of human quality of life are a function of consumption (see Figure 1.1). Those goods and services which sustain us, and make our lives easier or more pleasant, all require inputs of materials

---

Box 1.2 Six S's to Save the World!

Do you remember the three R's of education: reading, writing and arithmetic? Now it is time to learn about the six S's of sustainability.

- *Scale* The scale of the human economy must not exceed the capacity of the biosphere.
- *Solar* The power source of the future is the sun. Most human processes will need to be powered directly (or indirectly) by solar energy.
- *Cyclic (or 'S'yclic?)* If we do not reuse materials and recycle our wastes – mimicking the cyclical processes of nature – then we will deplete our resources and accumulate pollution.
- *Shared* A core principle of sustainability is that of equity. Nature's wealth should be shared rather than hoarded or appropriated by a minority.
- *Safe* No activity should compromise the health of plant or animal species, including people, by increasing the level of toxicity in the environment.
- *Sexy* No one wants to live in a world without fun!

With thanks to Edwin Datschefski, Biothinking International.[10]

and usage of natural sinks for waste products. From the economist's viewpoint, Paul Ekins has said 'what is destroyed by consumption is the value (from the human point of view) that was added in production'.[11]

The value or 'quality of life' we gain from consumption depends on a number of factors such as the sorts of activity we do (playing a game of cards is obviously less resource intensive than an outing in the car) and how efficient we are at converting materials into goods and services – one car might be more energy-efficient than another.

There is convincing evidence that above a certain threshold, further consumption adds little to reported quality of life.[12] For example, the percentage of Americans calling themselves 'happy' peaked in 1957 – even though consumption has more than doubled in the meantime.[13]

The cumulative environmental impact of any activity can be considered as a function of consumption levels. Where consumption patterns exceed nature's carrying capacity, locally or globally, then this is – by definition – unsustainable. In considering the impact of human consumption we need to be aware of both the number of consumers and the resource use associated with each activity.

Paul Ehrlich and John Holdren proposed the IPAT model where:[14]

Impact = Population x Affluence x Technology

This clearly shows the relationship between environmental impact, the number of consumers, the affluence – or level of consumption – of each consumer and the technological efficiency in delivering a particular product or service (see Box 1.3). We can simplify the model even further by considering consumption as the product of affluence and technology:

Impact = Population x Consumption

where consumption is the product of the efficiency with which the lifestyle activity is delivered. For example, the amount of fuel used to travel a certain distance depends on both the mode of transport and the efficiency of that form of travel.

To achieve ecological sustainability at a global level, 'impact' needs to be within the natural limits imposed by planetary carrying capacity. We consider this in greater detail in Chapters 3 and 4. For social sustainability, consumption patterns need to deliver at least a minimum quality of life for all.

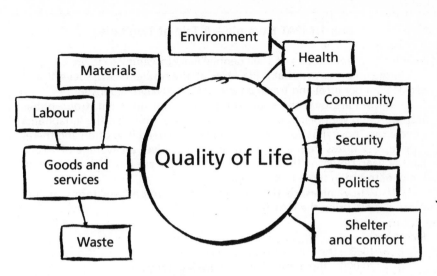

Figure 1.1 *Many aspects, though not all, of human quality of life are a function of consumption*

LINKING ECONOMICS, QUALITY OF LIFE AND THE ENVIRONMENT

Achieving sustainable development relies not only on the successful integration of social – quality of life – and environmental policies, but also on economic factors. How these so-called three 'pillars' fit together is the key. All too often we see the economy being treated as the sole 'bottom line' priority, in the mistaken belief that society and the environment exist to serve the economy rather than the other way around (see Figure 1.2a).

There is clearly a balance to be struck between the three elements. The phrase 'triple bottom line' is 'now embedded in the corporate lexicon world-wide'.[15,16] It is patently true that commerce cannot exist outside society, and society cannot exist outside the environment.

To reconcile and prioritize these three domains the authors are generally in agreement with the 'Russian Dolls' model of sustainability, proposed by Levett.[17] This places the economy in a more supportive position with social and environmental factors taking a more leading role (see Fig 1.2b).

The 'Russian Dolls' model proposes environmental sustainability as the real bottom line. Social objectives are achieved without damaging the environment – the economy exists to serve the needs of society in delivering quality of life. While at first glance this may seem a very anthropocentric viewpoint, it acknowledges the fact that both economy and society can, in the longer term, only exist within a healthy natural environment.

Box 1.3 IPAT Example – A Tale of Two Cities

Imagine two small towns of 1000 people: Blacktop and Parktown.

In the urban sprawl that is Blacktop, all the residents own fuel-efficient cars (15 km per litre) and travel an average of 20,000 km per year.

Over in Parktown the situation is somewhat different. Good public transport and well-planned amenities mean that only half the inhabitants need a car. Those that do own a car tend not to need it so often and therefore replace it less frequently. Each car-owner drives an average of 10,000 km per year. However, their older-model vehicles are less fuel efficient (10 km per litre) than those in Blacktop.

Let us now measure their environmental impact, in terms of fuel consumption, using the IPAT formula.

Blacktop
P = 1000 – the number of cars owned
A = 20,000 – the number of km travelled per year
T = 1/15 (or 0.0667) litres of fuel required per km
I = 1000 x 20,000 x 0.0667 = 1,334,000 litres (which corresponds to 3150 tonnes of CO_2) per year

Parktown
P = 500 cars
A = 10,000 km per year
T = 1/10 (or 0.1) litres per km
I = 500 x 10,000 x 0.1 = 500,000 litres (1181 tonnes of CO_2) per year

Thus despite having more fuel-efficient vehicles (Technology) the residents of Blacktop have a greater impact than those of Parktown due to both the number owning cars (Population) and their lifestyles which involve greater travel (Affluence or Lifestyle).

SUSTAINABILITY, SUSTAINABLE DEVELOPMENT, DEVELOPING SUSTAINABILITY – WHAT'S THE DIFFERENCE?

Some talk about 'sustainability', others say 'sustainable development' and then again we hear about 'developing sustainability'. If we are to make our progress sustainable, we need to understand where we are now, which direction we should be going in and how we will know when we have arrived.

Our starting point is to assume that the primary objective of sustainability is to achieve satisfying lives for all while staying within the bounds of nature. If either of these elements is not achieved then we will have failed in our efforts to reach sustainability.

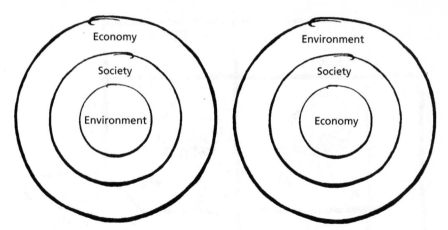

Figure 1.2 *Environment, society and economy: (a) the traditional view on the inter-relationship of economy, environment and society; (b) the 'Russian Dolls' model – where we want to be*

Using these elements we can classify different communities according to their position with respect to sustainability (see Figure 1.3).

In Figure 1.3, Zone A represents a situation where nature is protected but even the most basic quality-of-life objectives are not met. An example of this might be where a community has been denied access to natural resources and is therefore unable to feed, shelter or clothe itself, such as in the case of some wildlife conservation projects where the development needs of local people are ignored. While this may be ecologically sustainable, it is unlikely to be sustainable in human terms. A likely outcome is human suffering and conflict which will eventually erode both the social and natural environments.

Zone B represents a situation where both the environment is being degraded and quality of life is low (for example, poor public health). An example of this would be societies where poverty is endemic – where poverty results in further degradation, such as in the tragic case of Rwanda in the last few years. There are abundant cases where the overuse of fuel wood has led to deforestation or the over-extraction from community wells has led to loss of groundwater supplies.

Zone C represents a situation where people enjoy a satisfying quality of life, but where natural capital is not being adequately protected. Many Western societies fall into this category. They provide for a high standard of living, and possibly a high quality of life, but natural capital and the environment, either globally or locally, are being consumed or degraded. In many cases richer nations are able to protect their own environments by importing ecological capacity in an unsustainable manner.

Zone D is where both the key goals of sustainability are satisfied. A high quality of life is achieved without degrading the environment at

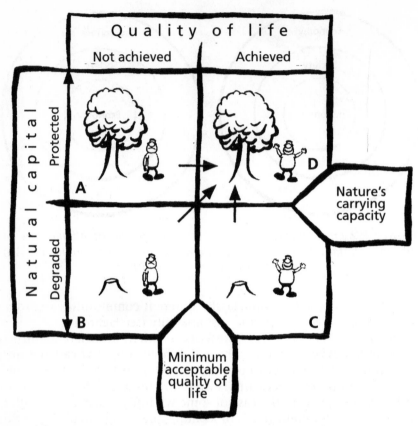

Figure 1.3 *Achieving quality of life within the means of nature; mapping out the process of achieving sustainability*

either the global or the local level. One notable example is the village of Gaviotas in Colombia (see Box 1.4).[18] Elsewhere eco-villages are flourishing. According to the Global Eco-village Network in Europe, these aim to provide 'solutions for meeting human needs, protection of the environment and an enhanced quality of life for all'. Their directory lists 57 eco-villages in 22 countries.[19]

Therefore, we can consider 'developing sustainability' as any move away from Zones A, B or C towards Zone D. Communities or societies in Zone D can be deemed 'sustainable communities'. Once a community is in Zone D, sustainable development, in terms of continuing to raise quality-of-life standards while protecting natural capital, becomes a reality.

For truly global sustainability, the global community needs to meet the criteria of Zone D where all people can lead satisfying lives and where nature is protected from overuse and abuse at both global and local levels.

Box 1.4 Gaviotas – A Village to Reinvent the World

Identified by the United Nations as a model village development and winner of the 1997 world prize in zero emissions from the UN Zero Emissions Research Initiative, Gaviotas is located in Colombia's hostile eastern savannahs – the llanos. Perhaps more than any other settlement, it has proved that social and ecological well-being are truly compatible partners.

This isolated community has frequently been referred to as a utopia, literally meaning 'no place', yet founder Paolo Lugari insists that Gaviotas is very much a real world 'topia'.

The village was founded in 1971 and is now home to around 200 Gaviotans. Before Gaviotas, apart from the Guahibo Indians, who eked out a meagre existence fishing and hunting along the narrow strips of fertile land bordering the rivers, and a few scattered ranchers, few lived in the grass-covered llanos. If people can live here they can live anywhere, Lugari thought.

The moving story of the settlement and development of the community, told by journalist Alan Weisman in his book *Gaviotas – A village to change the world* is an inspiring read.

The rain-leached soils of the llanos proved too barren to grow food so the resourceful Gaviotans introduced hydroponics suited to the location and based on available materials.

The problem of energy was solved by developing wind generators able to function in the light tropical breezes and designing buildings with vaulted roofs to collect solar radiation. Heating water to boiling point, vital in an area plagued by water-borne diseases, was achieved using a cleverly designed solar kettle. Cooking food required higher temperatures still and this was achieved by heating cottonseed oil in vacuum tubes exposed to the sun. Water was not readily available and had to be pumped from deep aquifers. Again, innovative thinking provided an answer in the development of a sleeve pump from a modified playground see-saw.

From the outset Gaviotas was conceived as a place which would offer a high quality of life. Somewhat reminiscent of early Israeli kibbutzim, schooling, housing, health care and food are free – there is no poverty and no crime. According to administrator Gonsalo Bernal, 'We have no police or jail, because nothing gets stolen. There is no need for laws or written rules. In Gaviotas, we just have codes of common sense.'

But perhaps the most startling achievement is the pine forest rising up around the village where little but rough grasses previously grew. A Honduran species was found to thrive in the harsh soils which, when mature, can be tapped for resin to make paint and turpentine. And in the shadow of the new trees, long-dormant seeds of native species are creating a lush habitat of laurels, ferns, horsetails, fig vines and many more – a total of 245 species at least. 'Elsewhere they're tearing down the rainforest,' says Weisman, 'but I've come to a place where they're actually putting it back.'

Source: see note 18

ENSURING QUALITY OF LIFE

How can we measure whether society is satisfied? Gross Domestic Product (GDP) is frequently (and misleadingly in the authors' opinion) used as a proxy measure of quality of life. GDP does indeed tell much about the level of consumption, but does it tell us anything about human welfare? We doubt it. By counting only monetary transactions, GDP omits much of what people value and that serves basic needs. Examples are all the unpaid services we provide: caring for children and the elderly, cooking, washing, and community volunteer work. It also ignores the value of time spent in recreation, relaxation and social activities.

Furthermore GDP omits the crucial contribution to the economy made by the natural environment – pure air and water, productive topsoil, moderate climate, and protection from the sun's harmful rays, for example. GDP takes no account of the depletion of natural resources used to produce goods and services. The harvesting of ancient redwood trees, for example, adds the market value of the wood to the economy.

GDP also fails to distinguish between monetary transactions that genuinely add to well-being and those that diminish it, try to maintain the status quo, or make up for degraded conditions. Much that contributes to economic growth is perceived by most people as loss rather than gain – fixing blunders from the past, borrowing from the future and shifting activities from the unpaid household or community sector to the monetized economy. For example, GDP treats crime, divorce, legal fees, and other signs of social breakdown as economic gains.

To address the inadequacies of GDP as a measure of sustainable income, attempts have been made to take account of depletion of capital (natural or man-made) and defensive expenditure on social disbenefits using a range of environmental evaluation techniques.[20]

Perhaps the most significant progress in this area is that made by Herman Daly, John Cobb and Cliff Cobb, who in 1989 devised a new measure which they called the Index of Sustainable Economic Welfare (ISEW).[21] In 1994, with Cliff Cobb's help, Redefining Progress, a San Francisco-based activist think-tank, further developed the ISEW into the Genuine Progress Indicator (GPI).[22] A major shortcoming of the GDP, which the GPI calculation rectifies, is its inability to distinguish between transactions that contribute to or diminish well-being. Therefore, GDP ends up looking like a business income statement that adds expenses to income instead of subtracting them. Since the GPI aims at documenting benefits, rather than merely tallying up spendings, it distinguishes between what most people perceive as positive and negative economic transactions, and between the costs of producing economic benefits and the benefits themselves.

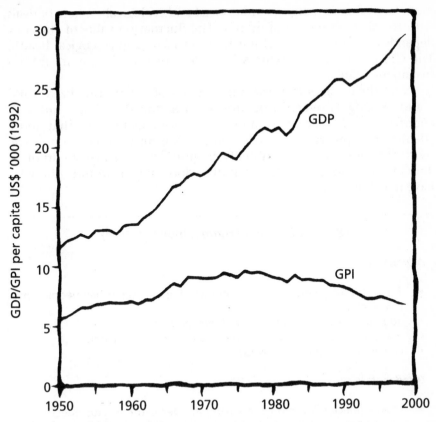

Figure 1.4 *GPI versus GDP in the US (1950–1999)*

The GPI adds up the value of products and services consumed in the economy – whether or not money changes hands. For example, it includes household work, parenting and volunteer work. Then it subtracts expenses that do not improve well-being – the defensive expenditures on crime, auto accidents, or pollution; social costs such as costs of divorce, crime, or loss of leisure time; and finally, the depreciation of environmental assets and natural resources, including loss of farmland, wetlands, and old growth forests, and the damaging effects of wastes and pollution. What it shows for the US is what most people feel: the net benefit of the economy is not rising as depicted by the GDP – rather the net benefit to people is in decline (see Figure 1.4).

Although the GPI can summarize key issues in one number, it has two shortcomings. First it mixes up the social and the ecological challenges of sustainability. Sustainability requires quality of life for all, *as well as* living within the means of nature – one should not be traded off against the other. Also, rather than providing a direct account of how things are, the GPI translates everything into money. This fails to acknowledge the complexities associated with assigning a meaningful monetary value to many essential social and ecological services or deals with the abstract nature of money. The fluctuating value of currency depends more on market whims than on social and ecological health. The GPI cannot easily express how close or how far we are from a sustainable state.

Nevertheless, money is the lingua franca of the industrialized world – and as long as overall measures such as the Dow Jones index or countries' GDP receive as much attention, using one that more adequately represents people's well-being is an effective step in the right direction. It is undoubtedly helping to open many corporate doors to the concept of sustainability, doors which would otherwise have remained firmly shut.

Box 1.5 Genuine Progress Indicator (GPI)

Advantages

- Translates into a measurement unit which industrial, urban people can easily relate to;
- aggregates everything into one single indicator;
- makes comparison simple between countries and over time;
- communicates very effectively.

Disadvantages

- Makes policies focus on the wrong answer if the wrong question is asked ('how much money is changing hands?' for the GDP, as opposed to the more meaningful question of 'what is the net benefit to people?' for the GPI);
- gives the impression of being an objective measure;
- mixes up social and ecological conditions; discounts the future;
- depends on valuation methods that do not produce consistent results.

WITHIN THE MEANS OF NATURE

We also need to define the point at which natural capital is degraded rather than protected; where we are living on nature's interest rather than living off nature's capital. A number of methodologies exist which rise to this challenge, as the next chapter explains. One way to tackle the measurement of nature's means is to compare consumption with the earth's carrying capacity using ecological footprint analysis. This is the focus of the remainder of this book.

SUMMARY

Our understanding of what constitutes real progress is changing. In this chapter we have explored the meaning of sustainability and identified its key components – environment, society and economy, and their relationship to one another. Furthermore, we have distinguished the aim of sustainability from the process of achieving sustainable development.

Using the IPAT formulation we have also introduced the role that population, lifestyle (or affluence), technology and consumption play in the measurement of environmental impact.

The authors have presented their preferred definition of sustainability which can be summarized as 'delivering quality of life for all within the means of nature'. This, and similar, definitions neatly capture the tension between these two key sustainability goals.

Defining in detail what constitutes a sufficient quality of life, and how this might be measured, is outside the scope of this book though the GPI, a candidate indicator, has been presented. What we are primarily concerned with in this book is how we might quantify our use of nature, and compare this with the carrying capacity of our ecosystems, so that we can assess environmental sustainability.

QUESTIONS

- Ecological footprinting deals only with measuring the 'means of nature'. This seems to ignore factors such as human health and the well-being of society. Aren't these important? (see Chapter 6, Question 9).
- Isn't sustainability about the triple bottom-line: environment, society and economy? You seem to ignore the economy (see Chapter 6, Question 10).
- Isn't there more to social needs than merely 'quality lives for all?' (see Chapter 6, Question 11).

NOTES

1   With thanks to Bill Rees for turning us in the direction of this quotation
2   McLaren, D, Bullock, S, Yousuf, N, 1998, *Tomorrow's World*, Earthscan, London
3   Department of the Environment, Transport and the Regions, 1998, *Opportunities for Change*, DETR
4   Conference speech 1998, Going for Green, London
5   Maria Sillanpää, The Body Shop, 'A New Deal for Sustainable Development in Business' in *Sustainable Measures*, ed, Bennett, P and James, P, 1999, Greenleaf, UK
6   Personal Communication, February 1999

7   Gore, A, 2000, *Earth in the Balance*, Earthscan, London
8   One is reminded of the 'Once-ler' in Dr Seuss' classic story of the Lorax. The Once-ler discovered a beautiful paradise and, ignoring the warnings of the wise Lorax, chopped down all the Truffler trees to make useless objects known as Thneeds. While the Once-ler and his family made a lot of money, before long the Truffler trees, the Lorax and the forest animals were gone, and the Once-ler's family had to move on. The Once-ler was left alone in the lifeless desert 'worrying with all his heart' and wishing for the return of the forest and the Lorax. (Dr Seuss, 1971, *The Lorax*, Collins Paperback Classics)
9   *Caring for the Earth, A Strategy for Sustainable Living*, 1991, UNEP, IUCN, WWF
10   http://www.biothinking.com. Last accessed December 1999
11   Zadek, S, Lingayah, S, and Murphy, S, 1997, *Purchasing Power – civil action for sustainable consumption*, New Economics Foundation
12   Carley, M and Spapens, P, 1998, *Sharing the World*, Earthscan, London
13   *Human Development Report 1998*, UNDP
14   Ehrlich, P and Holdren J, 1971, 'Impacts of population growth', *Science*, 171, pp1212–17 and Ehrlich, P and Holdren, J, 1972, 'One dimensional ecology', *Bulletin of Atomic Scientists*, 28 (5), pp16 and 18–21
15   Juniper, T, 2000, *Green Futures*, No 21, p54
16   http://www.sustainability.co.uk/triple, last accessed December 1999
17   Levett, R, 1998, *Journal of the Royal Statistical Society*, A 161
18   *Gaviotas – a village to re-invent the world*, 1998, by Alan Weisman, Chelsea Green Publishing. Transcripts of radio interviews with Weisman, 'Utopia Rises Out of the Colombian Plains' (broadcast by National Public Radio, 29 August 1994); 'Steve Curwood reports on Gaviotas' (broadcast by NPR on 1 May 1998) and 'Colombia's Model City' published by Context Institute in 1995 (http://www.context.org/ICLIB/IC42/Colombia.htm)
19   Gridheim, Kennedy and Komoch, 1998, *Directory of Eco-villages in Europe* GEN, Europe
20   Pearce, D, Markandya, A, Barbier, E, 1989, *Blueprint for a Green Economy*, Earthscan
21   Daly, H E and Cobb, J B, 1994, *For the Common Good*, Beacon Press
22   Cobb, C, Goodman, G, and Wackernagel, M, 1999, *Why Bigger Isn't Better: The Genuine Progress Indicator – 1999 Update*, Redefining Progress, San Francisco (downloadable PDF file from http://www.rprogress.org, or visit this site for more information on the GPI and links to comparable initiatives in other countries)

Chapter 2

Indicating Progress

'If you can't measure it you can't manage it' (Anon)

MEASURING WHAT WE VALUE

If we are to manage our way to sustainability, we must make the change from valuing what we measure to measuring what we value.

To track our progress down the road to sustainable development, it is necessary to be able to not only define, but also measure, the elements of sustainability – the bounds of nature, our impacts on it and our quality of life. Measuring any of the sustainability parameters in themselves – environmental, social and economic – is certainly not an easy task. Some critical data are not available, or cannot be readily compared with other places or times, and many essential qualities cannot simply be expressed in numbers.

Measurement is not the only problem. Even if we were able to accurately measure all sustainablility parameters, we would be presented with serious data overload and the data would be incomprehensible to all but the most focused specialists. This must somehow be reconciled with the reality that everyone has a role to play in achieving sustainability – whether it is in policy development or consumption decisions. To make the right decisions we all need credible, accessible and timely information. Hence the advent of the indicator.

WHAT MAKES A GOOD INDICATOR?

The Organization for Economic Cooperation and Development (OECD) definition of 'indicate' is to disclose or point out, to announce or make publicly known, or to estimate or put a price on.[1]

The packaging of data into indicators is a way of simplifying complex and detailed information.[2] This may be achieved in a variety

---

Box 2.1 What Makes a Good Indicator?

A good indicator must be:

Resonant – clear and easy to interpret and within the sphere of understanding and relevance of the user (national or local government, communities, organizations or individuals).

Valid – the data from which the indicator is drawn need to be as comprehensive and credible as possible (while noting that they should be easily accessible, and inexpensive to develop or obtain);[3] and the method used to develop the indicator must be as transparent as possible.

Motivational – reflecting issues that are within the sphere of influence of the user, so 'provoking and inspiring' change.[4] This should include the capacity to link to targets, show trends over time and cover issues that are deemed to be significant.

---

of ways – by choosing key topics, by omitting issues regarded as insignificant or by aggregation using weightings or conversion factors.

It is important that in the simplification process the credibility of the indicator is established and maintained. Care needs to be taken in ensuring that the indicators are drawn from a comprehensive data set, and that the method used for simplification is transparent – that value judgements or weighting methods are clearly explained.[5]

In addition, different audiences need to make different decisions – a national policy maker will need national indicators such as industrial CO_2 emissions; an individual may need a product indicator such as an 'ecolabel'. Box 2.1 shows a distillation of best practice in indicator development.

SUSTAINABILITY INDICATORS: AN INVITATION TO THE FAMILY GATHERING

> *'We think and act as if our economy, our environment, and our society's needs are at best unrelated realms. Sometimes we put them at odds with one another. We act as if environmental gains must bring economic losses, as if social gains must limit economic growth'* (Redefining Progress 1999).[6]

To derive useful sustainability indicators we need to look both at indicators of quality of life and at indicators for the health of the environment. As the World Resources Institute (WRI) points out, 'many highly aggregated economic and social indicators have been widely adopted, but there are virtually no comparable national environment indicators to help decision makers or the public evaluate environmental trends'.[7] Complex industrial systems mean that we often do not know the environmental implications of the goods and services we take for granted. As consumers, we know the price of a winter lettuce but we do not know, for example, how much energy went into its production and transportation. Companies vigilantly monitor and report profits and returns but only a few report on their greenhouse gas emissions.

But there is good news. The family of approaches to measure progress towards sustainability is growing. With all their differences, their messages are resonant in evaluating to what extent key sustainability challenges are met. Their goal is to document the pressure placed on the biosphere by people trying to lead satisfying lives. And, like in any family, every member has something special to contribute. Some approaches look at the process by focusing on the economy's contribution towards reaching these goals, or to what extent technologies have improved delivery of services with less impact. Let us introduce the diverse members of the family of sustainability indicators and describe their possibilities.

Indicator sets

With the rise of nation states with census data and increasing statistical capabilities, the use of statistics and corresponding indicators started to emerge as early as the late 19th century. While the search for social indicators experienced a peak in the 1970s, a renaissance of indicators has swept through the sustainability debate over the last ten years.[8]

'What is counted counts', summarizes the spirit of most indicator initiatives. The methodological twist of these initiatives is to go beyond a single number like GDP. Many communities, regions, states and even international organizations have launched indicator initiatives to propose a richer 'dashboard for the cockpit'. This broader set of indicators provides direct feedback on a multitude of social, ecological and economic aspects that shape a society's well-being. Rather than expressing everything in money, these indicators measure in direct units such as energy, number of recorded incidents, kilograms and percentage achievement, for example.

Indicator approaches over the last few years have been the most influential catalysts in advancing the debate on our future priorities. Many indicator initiatives have been successful in sparking discussions on key issues, highlighting trends and focusing society on its likes and dislikes. Nonetheless, many practitioners have become frustrated with the difficulties inherent in translating elaborate indicator reports into comprehensive public action. For example, global atmospheric concentrations of CO_2 tell the individual little or nothing about how they contribute to global warming.

LIVERPOOL
JOHN MOORES UNIVERSITY
AVRIL ROBARTS LRC
TITHEBARN STREET

Indicator activists have also started to recognize that broad indicator sets can diffuse debate, thus hindering the achievement of sustainability. Indicators can become bogged down in detail and miss the bigger picture. For example, the heated debate surrounding life cycle assessment methodologies focuses on calculating pollution impacts to the fifth decimal place, whereas even the most ball-park assessments of consumption show that we are hurtling, by far greater orders of magnitude, in the wrong direction.

In addition, complex indicator sets lead to confusion about achieving multiple goals. Too often the indicators remain disconnected – representing an ideal wish-list, but helping little to explain trade-offs or linkages between what happens at the global level compared with that at the local level. Few indicator initiatives incorporate the measurement, directly or indirectly, of ecological limits. For example, while the World Business Council for Sustainable Development's eco-efficiency indicator framework recognizes that this is necessary, no indicators to support the concept of carrying capacity have yet been developed.

As practitioners begin to recognize the limitations of conventional indicator initiatives, the questions arise as to how to sharpen the approach. Many approaches have failed to effectively move beyond gathering information. Much emphasis has been placed on the details, for example finding indicators for large numbers of issues facing a community. Consequently, many participants are overwhelmed with the long list of problems and the process gets bogged down. Any common sense of direction is eroded, the thrust of the indicator initiative weakens and the purpose becomes confounded. Participants become disenchanted since the effort results in little action.[9]

The next generation of indicators will most likely focus more specifically on their own underlying conceptual framework – they will move from being 'librarians' that organize information in categories to being 'plumbers' that focus on how the different categories are interconnected and what the trade-offs among them might be (see Figure 2.1).

The new indicators will most likely be:

- organized around a sharp purpose (for example, 'building municipal sustainability');
- captured in an effective framework for organizing the indicators that explains the challenges and trade-offs (for example, the framework could be the tension between securing quality of life versus maintaining the earth's biocapacity);
- imaginative and realistic about possible intervention points (for example, the focus of the campaign may be generating the public will rather than the 'planning ways'); and finally,
- specific about the next steps beyond the indicators project before even starting it (for example, a specific follow-up may be to engage the municipality in issues of tax reform in order to implement comprehensive sustainability ideas).

Figure 2.1 *Indicators must move from being librarians to plumbers*

Various frameworks have already been developed that help organize sustainability indicators. Earlier ones were arranged around the function of the indicators. For example, the widely used 'pressure–state–response' framework divides indicators into those that cause an outcome (the emission of air pollutants for example), those that document the outcome (the state of smog) and those that react to the outcome (the air pollution legislation that is in place as a response). All these indicator types play significant roles: the pressure indicators are necessary to predict what kind of pressures we may expect and state indicators are necessary to judge the success of responses to those pressures. Other organizations have focused more on arranging the indicators according to sustainability challenges to make sure all core concerns are adequately covered. Over the next few pages we examine in detail the most prominent current applications of indicators to the measurement of sustainability.

The Natural Step: a Framework for Sustainability

Humans depend on the ecosphere – that part of the earth that supports life. Therefore, they put themselves at risk if they systematically alter the biophysical conditions of the ecosphere. Examples of such disruptions are the systematic increases in the atmosphere's concentration of CO_2, the concentrations of metals and human-made chemicals in soil and water, and the decrease in areas of productive soils and fresh water. Starting from these fundamental and different ways for a society to destroy the functions of the ecosphere, The Natural Step, an organization founded by Karl-Henrik Robèrt, developed four principles for sustainability.[10] They maintain that in order for a society to be sustainable, nature's functions and diversity must not be systematically:

- subject to increasing concentrations of substances extracted from the earth's crust;
- subject to increasing concentrations of substances produced by society;
- impoverished by over-harvesting or other forms of ecosystem manipulation such as decreasing the thickness of the productive soils, nutrient contents, groundwater, genetic variation etc.

Together, the first three principles give a framework for ecological sustainability, which implies a set of restrictions within which sustainable societal activities must be incorporated. Based on that reasoning, a first-order principle for the society's internal turnover of resources is formulated – the fourth principle:

- resources are used fairly and efficiently in order to meet basic human needs worldwide.

These principles provide a powerful framework for organizing indicators – and have been applied in both business and governmental contexts.[11]

Box 2.2 The Natural Step

Advantages

- Provides a simple approach that is easy to imitate;
- displays desegregated information;
- links ideas, concerns and policies directly to specific measures;
- can get started without agreement on underlying causes;
- is educational and helps in building coalitions.

Disadvantages

- Does not give an understanding of the systemic drivers that move society towards unsustainable behaviour;
- can get lost in details, which easily leads initiatives off track and detracts from action;
- can promote wishful thinking in the absence of acknowledging trade-offs;
- is not standardized.

Environmental Space: Targets for Sustainability

'Environmental space' is a methodology for achieving sustainability. It is a set of resource consumption indicators first proposed by Johan Opshoor and then developed by Friends of the Earth. As well as showing current status, these indicators are linked to a sustainable benchmark value for each indicator. In other words, it is one of the few indicator approaches that not only documents the amounts of ecological capacity used by people, but also the amounts that could be used in a sustainable world. It is essentially a 'distance to target' approach where sustainable use for key environmental resources is defined as a global target for sustainability. Once the 'environmental space' for those key resources has been defined, they are expressed as global per capita 'quotas' in line with a set of 'equity principles' of sustainable development. For example, assuming a global target of 11.1 gigatonnes CO_2 emissions is required to maintain climate stability by 2050, and assuming that global population in 2050 is 9.8 billion, the per capita 'environmental space' for energy is 1.1 tonnes per year.[12] UK per capita production of CO_2 is in the region of 9 tonnes, thus implying a reduction in UK emissions by about 85 per cent. So far, Friends of the Earth have completed similar calculations for construction materials, metals, land and wood.

The environmental space concept has many commendable aspects. It is useful in communicating the issues surrounding 'fair shares' and equitable access to resources, and effective in expressing the 'per capita' implications of implementing a set of global environmental protection policies. It does however have a number of weaknesses. An in-depth analysis of the strengths and the weaknesses of environmental space is given in *The Concept of Environmental Space* by John Hille.[13] We outline some of the issues here.

Firstly, rather than being an indicator which could help to set global targets, it relies on a predefined 'sustainability state' and preset estimates of environmental space. Some might argue that these are subjective estimates. For example, the global environmental space target for chlorine is set at zero and a complete phase out of chemical fertilizer products is prescribed.[14]

Secondly, environmental space takes little account of the interactions between different types of resources. Environmental space targets for non-fuel minerals are based on the comprehensive and detailed work done on material intensity per unit of service (MIPS) at the Wuppertal Institute by Schmidt-Bleek. Targets are set at a 50 per cent reduction in material input. As we point out later, the MIPS methodology makes no attempt to compare the consequences of inputs of different types of material, simply representing total amount of materials moved in the course of economic activity, as a proxy for environmental damage. For example, the contribution towards eco-sustainability of a 50 per cent reduction in global aluminium consumption by weight might be considerably greater than a 50 per cent reduction in steel consumption. This problem of how to add the 'apples and pears' of environmental demands is a common one.

Similarly, this concept defines an environmental space target for agricultural land, forest land and land for construction, but does not attempt to make any links between differing uses of what is essentially the same resource. Without taking an overall view of issues such as land use, it is not possible to use the method to develop useful scenarios of sustainability. As with some of the other indicators, there is a risk of double counting impacts providing a potentially misleading picture. In Chapter 4 we outline further the competing demands for land use.

Thirdly, the concept of environmental space uses a 'top–down' approach. Although helpful in guiding policy decisions at the global and national levels, it does not lend itself to linking the environmental consequences of our lifestyle decisions to the global sustainability issue. To make environmental space targets meaningful to the individual, they would need to be expressed on an activity-to-'fair share' basis, impacts being measured with a life cycle approach. For example, how much of one's fair share of land is appropriated by eating a banana!

Fourthly, there are problems in defining the boundaries used for determining sustainability targets. This again is a common problem. In *Towards Sustainable Europe* (Friends of the Earth, 1995), environmental space targets for mineral resources are set on a global basis on the grounds that minerals are a globally traded resource. Targets for agricultural products on the other hand are set at the continental level. This makes it difficult to consistently take account of global equity issues.

Box 2.3 Environmental Space

Advantages

- Sets targets for sustainability over different time horizons;
- conveys concepts and realities of equity and distributive justice;
- useful for national policy-makers in setting targets and checking progress.

Disadvantages

- Targets are set on 'best estimates' and do not always take into account properties of different materials;
- does not convey interactions between usage of different resources and materials substitution;
- difficult to make resonant to the individual.

Systems models

With the advent of rapidly growing computing power, tools have been developed that can model the behaviour of complicated systems. Since the launch of *World3* by Donella Meadows, Dennis Meadows, Jørgen Randers and their colleagues, as described in their influential book *Limits to Growth* and the sequel *Beyond the Limits*,[15] the interest in modelling complex systems has been steadily on the rise. Most attempts have tried to capture social, economic and ecological interactions in order to explore possible outcomes of current decisions.

While these models have powerful possibilities to enhance our understanding of the world, their results are easily discredited. Often they are dismissed on the grounds that the model is a 'black box' with no transparency. And indeed, it is impossible to explain the model with a few one-liners. Critics take advantage of that, and in order to discredit the results, they claim that the links modelled in the system are built on speculative assumptions. In other words, with the cultural bias against such models and the difficulty of explaining the thinking behind a model in succinct ways, it is hard to build wide support for acting on the results. This is particularly the case if the results point to uncomfortable conclusions that are in contradiction to our wishful expansionary thinking.

Nevertheless, modelling is becoming a more common tool among resource managers – not only to understand forest fires or fisheries dynamics, but probably most prominently in analysing potential consequences and patterns of global climate change.

Box 2.4 Systems Models

Advantages

- Helps in thinking systemically about issues;
- can handle complex problems of interactions;
- helps in predicting and identifying likely scenarios and impacts of policy choices;
- can produce high levels of predictive power when used with a scientific consensus process (for example climate models);
- provides effective educational support; and
- is useful in sharpening the thinking of the researchers.

Disadvantages

- Weak for building public support;
- can easily be misunderstood and misinterpreted;
- the quality of model is hard to assess from outside; and
- is vulnerable to unfriendly criticism.

LIVERPOOL JOHN MOORES UNIVERSITY
LEARNING SERVICES

Environmental Impact Assessment and Critical Loads

In 1969, the US took a lead in institutionalizing environmental impact assessments. Congress legislated that all government projects needed from thereon to be subject to a formal assessment of potential impacts. Soon other countries followed suit.

While this regulatory approach was a bold step forward, environmental impact statements have not been able to rigorously address the systematic increase of ecological pressure by industrialized countries. There is no doubt, however, that these countries have been pushed to improve their local resource management and into more effective pollution prevention than if these regulations did not exist.

Nevertheless, environmental impact assessments are plagued by many weaknesses. Since the format, and the definition of what constitutes a related impact, can vary, the studies are often so detailed that it becomes impossible to draw an overall conclusion. Also, all of them struggle with capturing not only direct, but also indirect effects of projects. For example, in the case of a bridge, these studies should not merely include the immediate physical impact of constructing the bridge, but also the even larger impact of the increased volume of traffic the new bridge will attract.

Furthermore, impact assessments hardly ever incorporate cumulative effects of projects. They only analyse each project on its own merits, ignoring whether all the existing projects together are already exceeding the carrying capacity of the affected ecosystems. For example, even though a project may pump less acidity into the atmosphere than similar projects in the region, the new project, together with all existing projects, may still contribute to excessive levels of acid rain. In consequence, even low-impact projects will eventually surpass overall limits if there are too many of them. This is a recurring theme with existing environmental indicators, including life cycle assessment and corporate environmental performance evaluation (see next section).

Psychologically, framing environmental concerns in terms of 'impacts' has also been a limitation of the method. Rather we should see environmental destruction as a loss of benefits. By expressing environmental concerns as impacts, the environment becomes an 'additional cost factor' and people forget that the environment is really the origin of all benefits – which are diminished through human impacts. Learning from this shortcoming, newer environmental initiatives emphasize the benefits and talk about positive ecological functions and services – and point out their overuse.

Nevertheless, this regulatory approach has also led to the establishment of pollution standards. For example, by starting to define critical loads for a number of waste substances, there is now a more specific criterion to determine to what extent potentially toxic substances are leading to unacceptable levels of substance concentration in the environment. Many of these critical loads may be driven by immediate human health concerns, which are important, but may ignore their potential to accumulate over time and the long term impact of these substances on future generations.

Box 2.5 Environmental Impact Assessment and Critical Loads

Advantages

- Legally required in many countries and for many projects;
- provide detailed descriptions of possible impacts.

Disadvantages

- Provide little standardized information;
- make people 'drown' in details;
- provide too many loopholes to circumvent legal requirements;
- have had little success in mitigating overall impacts;
- ignore cumulative effects; and
- confuse human health and ecological health.

Corporate Environmental Performance Evaluation

The international standard ISO 14031 provides a framework for environmental performance evaluation (EPE) based on environmental condition indicators, management performance indicators, and operational performance indicators. Some of the suggested operational performance indicators are normalized per unit of product or service,[16] to give resource intensities, which is a necessary step in linking corporate eco-efficiency to both final consumption and ecological capacity. Spangenberg points out that resource intensities should ideally cover energy intensity, materials intensity and land use intensity.[17] While energy intensity is a better known corporate performance indicator, few if any cover the latter categories, focusing instead on output indicators such as pollution levels.

The World Business Council on Sustainable Development is also developing work on eco-efficiency indicators and take their definition of eco-efficiency further than ISO 14031. They define eco-efficiency as 'the delivery of competitively priced goods and services that satisfy human need and bring quality of life, while progressively reducing ecological impacts and resource intensity throughout the life cycle, to a level at least in line with the earth's estimated carrying capacity'.[18]

This is a relatively new approach to indicators and as yet few organizations have taken up the challenge of this sort of evaluation.[19]

The bk doesn't
pressurise businesses or
make them feel bad if they
don't.

For most organizations environmental performance data are still expressed in terms of the organization or site rather than the products it produces – for example, total CO_2 emissions or litres of water used – though interesting work by DuPont in Wilmington, in the US, expresses some of its performance data in terms of energy and materials intensity per unit of product. The flooring company 'Interface' is also making progress in this direction.[20] These values could be used in the same way as life cycle analysis (LCA) to indicate the amount of embodied resources in a particular product or service,[21] thereby overcoming the common problem of relating environmental demands of particular products to global ecological capacity.

The Global Reporting Initiative provides a similar framework in an attempt to standardize sustainability reporting for corporations.[22]

Box 2.6 Corporate Environmental Performance Evaluation

Advantages

• Illustrates materials and energy intensity of production and services; and
• can link use of nature to value created.

Disadvantages

• No standard reporting framework;
• does not illustrate cumulative effects or link to global ecological capacity; and
• does not aggregate ecological impacts.

Life Cycle Analysis

One of the most used, but little standardized, approaches to assess impacts of products and processes is LCA. It provides detailed accounts of all the energy, resources and waste materials associated with a product over its entire life cycle.

In order to avoid value judgements, many of these studies do not provide a summary statement. In consequence, these studies provide the information of impacts in much detail, identifying the direct and indirect resources it uses and the wastes it generates. Nevertheless, many indirect effects are hard to capture and they rely on assumptions. Also, with the need to track products over their whole life, and the details one needs to know for each specific product (including, for example, the electric power composition of the electricity bought by the manufacturing plant), these assessments become very labour intensive. Their results also remain hard to interpret since they are not aggregated. The models that do attempt to aggregate, to a single figure such as in the EcoPoints methodology, use distance to target weight-ings[23] or weightings agreed by a panel of experts,[24] and are hence subjective and not always transparent.

Nevertheless, for other assessment methods, LCAs provide a wealth of data which could be used to explore the links between consumption of particular products and global biocapacity.

Box 2.7 Life Cycle Analysis

Advantages

- The provision of detailed descriptions of impacts; and
- does not aggregate.

Disadvantages

- Provides little standardized information;
- makes people 'drown' in details;
- ignores cumulative effects; and
- confuses human health and ecological health.

Material Accounts: MIPs and Regional Metabolisms

Metabolic studies and material accounts have witnessed probably the most rapid advances in the field of sustainability metrics. Among the advocates of this method are Peter Baccini from the Swiss Federal Institute and Paul Brunner from the Technical University in Vienna, who have developed powerful methodologies to trace stocks and flows of various materials through industrialized regions. These flows have highly practical applications when determining how to reduce overall emission of persistent toxins such as heavy metals, or how to restore the nitrogen balance of industrial societies. Work on total materials flows (TMF) of industrial economies highlights a range of resource flow issues such as the hidden flows associated with production and consumption.[25]

Friedrich Schmidt-Bleek originated another approach to material accounting at the Wuppertal Institute which he named material intensity per unit of service (MIPS) This can be applied more directly to industrial processes and products. Essentially, MIPS combines life cycle analysis and material accounting to determine the overall mass transformed for a given process – from cradle to grave. 'Rather than focusing on the nanograms [of pollution], we need to focus on the megatonnes [of resource use]' he explained,[26,27] and basic thermodynamics is on his side. Since matter does not disappear, material accounts are ideal for tracing flows through human society and industrial economies.

But the interpretation of the results remains ambiguous. What is the maximum amount of mass that can be transformed sustainably? We may be in danger of 'weighing our wallets to see how much money we have'.[28] Does each kilogram of mass indeed have similar enough impacts in order to aggregate them without any weighting? It is hardly the case that one kilogram of water being moved by a sailing boat would cause as much impact as one kilogram of fuel to power the boat. Nevertheless, MIPS offers a good first approximation of the magnitude of human impact and helps to measure relative improvements over time.

Box 2.8 Material Accounts: MIPS and Regional Metabolisms

Advantages

- Build rigorous accounting systems using the law of 'conservation of matter';
- metabolic studies provide crucial inputs for management systems.

Disadvantages

- Provide no information about the maximum sustainable impact that can be allowed
- assume that each kilogram of mass transformed has the same ecological impact.

Energy and 'eMergy' analysis

There is a high correlation between people's use of energy and their destructive ecological power. Thus it makes sense to consider using energy as a proxy measure for overall environmental impact. Thanks to the first law of thermodynamics on the conservation of energy, which means that the energy input to a system must eventually be the same as the system's energy output, energy is also an ideal unit for accounting. And indeed, over the last 100 years, several energy-based economics and energy analyses have been developed to elaborate the dynamics of industrial systems.

Particularly noteworthy is HT Odum's 'eMergy' approach, which translates all activities into the energy required to make the activity happen. All such embodied energy stems eventually from the sun. Odum termed this embodied energy 'eMergy' or 'energy memory', referring to it as the 'currency of nature and society'. Odum uses 'eMergy' to describe interactions between humans and nature.[29]

Another ever more popular approach is to use the biosphere's net primary productivity (measured in megajoules per year) as the energy currency. This allows us to compare human use of biomass to the biosphere's overall capacity to produce biomass. Peter Vitousek and his colleagues calculated for 1980, based on very conservative assumptions, that humanity was at that time already appropriating 40 per cent of the terrestrial ecosystem production (and this did not include the need for absorbing CO_2 from fossil fuel).[30] More recent initiatives building on this approach have been initiated by Marina Fischer-Kowalski and her colleagues at the University of Vienna.[31]

Box 2.9 Energy and 'eMergy' Analysis

Advantages

- Provides a good proxy measure of overall impact;
- ideal for rapid appraisals of industrial processes.

Disadvantages

- Availability of data for some types of energy analysis (particularly 'eMergy') is weak;
- some forms of energy analysis provide no insight into upper limts on the use of nature;
- integration of non-renewable and renewable energy is not developed;
- typically ignores risk and toxicity.

COMPLETING THE FAMILY: THE IDEAS BEHIND THE ECOLOGICAL FOOTPRINT

The family of indicators described needs to be complemented by one that shows the overall environmental impact of humanity. The basic ecological question for sustainability is, how much nature do we have as compared with how much nature we use? Since it is theoretically possible to use nature's materials and services more rapidly than nature can regenerate them, the prime condition for ecological sustainability is to make sure, at the very least in quantitative terms, that such overshoot does not occur. That is, the scale of the economy must not exceed the scale of the biosphere. If this were to be the case, the ecological assets of this planet would be depleted and qualitative improvement alone would be insignificant in moving us towards sustainability.

Imagine the planet as an open-topped water butt – the liquid representing our resources. The butt can only be replenished by the steady dripping of resources from solar energy. To avoid depleting planetary natural capital we must live off the overflow and not run the barrel dry. Our 'technological tap' should be placed at the top rather than at the base (see Figure 2.2).

Figure 2.2 *The water butt analogy*

Apart from having a tool that gives a summary of the overall use of nature (as compared with its regenerative capacity), would it not also be useful to have an assessment tool that captures people's impacts without alienating them through judgement? One that challenges the public to make choices themselves by not allocating implicitly or explicitly quotas or consumption rights to given population groups? One that does, however, link personal activities to global biocapacity? How about one that does not build on speculative assumptions about people's future behaviour, future technological possibilities, or particular policy paths? Or one that does not require an understanding about the causal relationships between the various aspects influencing sustainability of today's events but just accounts for the outcome? How about a tool that captures the contribution of both consumption and population?

These are some of the aspirations that the ecological footprint brings to the family of indicators described in this chapter. The remainder of this book looks at the various uses, strengths and weaknesses of the ecological footprint.

FOOTPRINTING IN A NUTSHELL

In essence, the ecological footprint is a simple accounting tool that adds up human impacts (or use of ecological services) in a way that is consistent with thermodynamic and ecological principles. It goes beyond capturing biomass appropriation by also including ecological services such as waste absorption or water use. Footprint analysis captures the use of nature in as far as it impacts on the regenerative capacity of the biosphere. It expresses these ecological impacts in units of space. In other words, it measures how much nature, expressed in the common unit of 'bioproductive space with world average productivity', is used exclusively for producing all the resources a given population consumes and absorbing the waste they produce, using prevailing technology.

The footprint intentionally says nothing about people's quality of life. Quality of life has to be looked at separately, as the last chapter pointed out. In the remainder of this book the authors consider only ecological outcomes, independent of the reasons or mechanisms that caused them, and identify who contributes how much to the overall impact. The authors have tried to avoid speculation about future possibilities or the dynamics underlying the current situation. Also, in order not to exaggerate the severity of the present situation, footprint results underestimate the true overall impact and exaggerate the biocapacity that exists on the planet. In this sense the footprint is not a precise model of how the biosphere works. Rather it provides a utilitarian view of nature – nature as a big bucket filled with resources – and measures who takes what. It can, however, be used to illuminate how much 'value' we get from our use of nature.

Using such a crude simplification of nature is also a strategic feature of the model. It makes it appeal more to those reluctant to accept the ideas of ecological constraints (let us say resource economists) while still getting support from other sectors of society with opposing world views (let us say deep ecologists or people in the nature conservancy movement). Also, since it can be applied independently of geographic scale (from the globe down to the personal) and since it talks in graphic language, it communicates effectively and resonates with the experiences of many people.

As we develop this tool further, we aim to ensure that it remains as robust as possible and focuses on those aspects that truly limit the biosphere's regenerative capacity. By keeping it static rather than dynamic and by making it underestimate the true ecological impact of humanity, we trust that the ecological footprint will avoid falling into the trap of some of its more speculative family members. Step forward to the possibilities of footprinting.

QUESTIONS

- What is the advantage of aggregating different environmental impacts into one indicator? (see Chapter 6, Question 1)
- Isn't the footprint just another arbitrary sustainability index? (see Chapter 6, Question 2)
- Isn't the footprint a bit too simplistic? (see Chapter 6, Question 3)
- What's the advantage of simplifying so much? (see Chapter 6, Question 4)
- Has ecological footprinting got anything to do with local Agenda 21? (see Chapter 6, Question 15).

NOTES

1   OECD, 1998, *Towards sustainable development, Environmental Indicators,* OECD
2   Adriaanse, A, 1995, *Accounting for Change,* New Economics Foundation 1995
3   Pearce, Bill, 1997, *Using indicators to guide policy and measure progress towards a sustainable region,* Presentation to Signs of the Times conference TCPA Lancaster University
4   Royal Borough of Kensington and Chelsea, 1998, *State of the Environment: Sustainability Indicators Report*
5   Hammond, A, et al, undated, 'Environmental Indicators: a systematic approach to measuring and reporting on environmental policy performance' in *The Context of Sustainable Development,* WRI
6   http://www.rprogress.org

7   Hammond, A, et al, op cit
8   See http://iisd1.iisd.ca/measure for a compendium of indicator projects
9   Cobb, C W, and Rixford, C, November, 1998, *Lessons from the history of social indicators*, Redefining Progress, San Francisco. Downloadable as a PDF File from http://www.rprogress.org/pubs/publist.html
10   For more information, read John Holmberg, Karl-Henrik Robèrt, and Karl-Erik Eriksson, 1996, 'Socio-Ecological Principles for a Sustainable Society: Scientific Background and Swedish Experience' in Costanza, R, Olman, S and Martinez-Alier, J (eds) *Getting Down to Earth*, pp17–48 (Washington, Island Press). Or visit www.naturalstep.org, the website of the US branch of the organization
11   For more specific examples of how indicators can be linked to the framework, consult Christian Azar, John Holmberg, and Karen Lindgren, 1996, 'Socio-ecological indicators for sustainability', *Ecological Economics*, vol 18, no 2, pp89–112. The relationship of footprints with these systems conditions is discussed in John Holmberg, Ulrika Lundqvist, Karl-Henrik Robèrt and Mathis Wackernagel, 'The Ecological Footprint from a Systems Perspective of Sustainability', *The International Journal of Sustainable Development and World Ecology*, vol 6, pp17–33, 1999
12   McLaren, D, Bullock, S, Yousuf, N, 1998, *Tomorrow's World*, Earthscan
13   Hille, J, 1998, *The Concept of Environmental Space – Implications for policies, environmental reporting and assessments*, EEA
14   Friends of the Earth, 1995, *Towards Sustainable Europe*
15   Meadows, D H, Meadows, D L, and Randers, J, 1992, *Beyond the Limits*, Earthscan
16   International Standards Organisation, 1999, 'ISO 14031: Environmental management – environmental performance evaluation guidelines'
17   Spangenberg, J H, and Bonniot, O, 1999, *Sustainability Indicators – A compass on the Road towards Sustainability*, Wuppertal Institute
18   WBSCD, January 1999, 'Eco-efficiency value creation through innovation and efficiency improvement', Bulletin
19   As are most materials-flow-based indicators. See Spangenberg, J H, Femia, A, Hinterberger, F, Schutz, H October, 1998, *Materials Flow-based Indicators in Environmental Reporting*, European Environment Agency
20   Interface Sustainability Report, 1997, Interface, Inc., Atlanta
21   Carberry, J, March 1999, Conference speech 'Towards a common framework for corporate sustainability reporting', Imperial College, London, 4–5 March
22   See www.globalreporting.org
23   Goedkoop, M, Demmers, M, Collignon, M, 1995, *The Eco-Indicator 95*, Pre Consultants, Amersfoort, The Netherlands
24   Alan Yates, Building Research Establishment UK, Personal Communication, 1999
25   World Resources Institute, *Resource Flows: The Material Basis of Industrial Economies*, 1997
26   Schmidt-Bleek, F, 1994, *Wieviel Umwelt braucht der Mensch? MIPS Das Maß fürökologisches Wirtschaften* (How much nature do people need? MIPS a measure for ecological management), Birkhäuser Verlag, Basel
27   *Fresenius Environmental Bulletin*, vol 2, no 8, Special edition on Material Intensity per Unit of Service (MIPS) project of the Wuppertal Institute für Klima, Umwelt, und Energie Wuppertal, Germany 1993

28 Oliver Tickell, personal communication
29 Odum, H T, 1994, *Ecological and General Systems*, Revised edition, University of Colorado Press, Boulder
30 Vitousek, Peter M, Paul R Ehrlich, Ann H Ehrlich and Pamela A Mateson, 1986, 'Human Appropriation of the Products of Photosynthesis', *BioScience*, vol 34, no 6, pp368–373
31 See for example, Helmut Haberl, 1997, 'Human Appropriation of Net Primary Production as an Environmental Indicator: Implications for Sustainable Development', *Ambio*, vol 26, no 3, pp143–146

Chapter 3

Footprinting Foundations

'We need nature more than nature needs us' (Sadruddin Aga Khan, spiritual leader of the Ismaili sect of Shiite Muslims, 1991)

Though ecological footprinting has only been around since 1990,[1] the foundations of the concept can be traced back through several threads of literature and research drawing on ecology, economics and geography. A basic knowledge of some of the relevant issues within these disciplines is helpful, if not essential, to an understanding of the methodology itself.

In this chapter the authors present the key topics of land resources and carrying capacity, and introduce several other related ideas by way of brief summaries and references.

LAND AS A FINITE RESOURCE

'The problem with land is that they stopped making it some time ago' (Attributed to Mark Twain)

Land Services

Our connection to land is primal – it features strongly in our day-to-day living and in our cultural history. We walk on it, grow things in it, build on it, fight for it and admire it. People will work hard for many years just so that they can buy or rent a little patch of it to call their home.

Land speculation and accumulation have become integral to the workings of most economies, yet this financial emphasis masks the many other ecological and social services that land provides 'for free':[2]

- Production based on plant growth – food, animal fodder, fibres, timber, fuelwood.
- Regulation of the atmospheric and hydrological cycles.
- Conservation of biodiversity and habitats: plant and animal species, ecosystems, genetic resources.
- Storage and ongoing supply of non-renewable resources: fuels, minerals, and non-biotic raw materials.
- Functions related to human settlement: housing, industry, transportation, recreation.
- Waste disposal: receiving, filtering and transforming the waste products of settlements.
- Heritage – preserving sites of interest and beauty, and evidence of cultural history.

In recent years the use of satellites, and other technical advances, have greatly added to our knowledge of global land types and trends.[3] It is no longer a matter of understanding the extent of our land resources but an issue of their management.

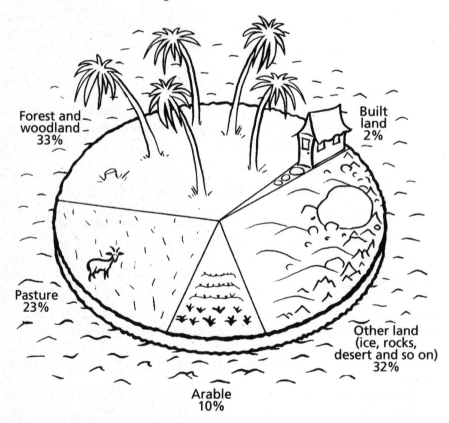

Note: see text for data on land areas

Figure 3.1 *Global land resources*[7]

Global Land Use

Our land resources are finite. The surface area of the planet is about 51 billion ha, most of which is water. Less than 15 billion ha of this is land.[4] The Food and Agricultural Organization (FAO) of the UN collates data about global land use.[5] The classifications are broad and subject to alteration, reflecting the variable quality and reliability of the data available. Based on this, and other sources, the authors have broadly categorized global land resources (see Figure 3.1).[6]

Land use statistics indicate that about 1.5 billion ha, or 10 per cent of the total global land area, is arable. This is defined as land under temporary and permanent crops, which covers everything from rice to rubber – although it excludes land used to grow trees for fuelwood or timber.[8]

Looking in more detail at the use of this cropland, almost half (48 per cent) is used to grow cereal crops. The rest is a mixture of other staples. Overall, the world's population depends on just 30 crops for 95 per cent of its food. Together just four crops – wheat, rice, maize and potatoes – account for a bigger share than all the other crops combined.

Around 3.4 billion ha (23 per cent) are classified as permanent pasture. This category, mostly used for beef and mutton production, is perhaps the most difficult to define and reporting errors are common.[9] It is generally used to refer to land used for five or more years for forage including natural and cultivated crops.

A further 5.1 billion ha (33 per cent) are referred to as forest and woodland. Of this approximately 3.4 billion ha are tropical, temperate and boreal forests. The remaining 1.7 billion ha consist of lightly wooded areas – some of it with as little as 10 per cent tree cover.[10]

Much of the remaining 5 billion ha is wetlands, ice, rocks, desert, tundra, lakes and rivers.[11] This broad category includes around 0.3 billion ha of built land.[12]

Adding together the figures for arable, pasture and built land gives us a rough indication of the area of the globe which has been heavily modified to provide for humanity. The figure works out at above 35 per cent – an amount which is predicted to rise significantly in the next 50 years, pushing back the boundaries of the remaining natural areas.[13]

Various estimates put the total area of bio-productive land at somewhere between 8.7 and 10.3 billion ha.[14] This wide range reflects differences in land classification systems. In this text the authors use the higher, more optimistic estimate.

Trading Land

Land use patterns vary enormously as a result of both human activity and climatic conditions. For example, Asia has only one third as much forested land (18 per cent of its total land area) as South America (53 per cent). The proportion of land given over to crops is more similar, as one would expect, yet the range is still quite large: 17 per cent of Asia is cropland compared with about 6 per cent for Oceania.[15]

One key factor influencing land use patterns is international trade. No longer do countries provide merely for their own population, but act as players in the global marketplace. This is particularly apparent with foodstuffs, the top five traded commodities being cereals, sugar, coffee, cocoa and bananas.

Typically, high-income, densely populated or resource-poor regions rely on appropriating, or 'importing', land outside of their own boundaries to provide them with the products that they desire. Such trade is used to both bolster, or substitute for, local production and to secure items that are not provided locally – minerals, materials, consumer goods and foodstuffs, for example.[16] A report by Friends of the Earth Europe looked at the total 'import' and 'export' of embodied pasture and arable land from the European Union (EU) calculated from the data on yields and tonnages of traded animal and vegetable products. Interestingly, whilst the EU is a substantial net importer of land, it maintains a positive financial trade balance in agricultural products,[17] suggesting that a higher value is placed on the land that is exported than that which is imported.

As the globalization of our economy leads to regions becoming more interdependent, the health of distant ecosystems becomes the concern of us all. Donella H Meadows uses the thought-provoking term 'global village' to describe this phenomenon[18] – an idea which the authors have developed further in linking global land use issues to local circumstances.[19]

Of particular concern is the evidence that current use of the global land resource is environmentally unsustainable. Significant degradation is occurring in all regions of the world.[20,21,22] Three main causes of human-induced land degradation – overgrazing, deforestation and other agricultural mismanagement – have been identified. In some regions of Asia, Africa and Europe, more than one-fifth of the total vegetated land is affected. The situation has deteriorated further in recent years with a further 5 to 6 million ha being severely degraded annually.[23] Land area alone does not tell the whole story. Urbanization, a more minor cause of degradation when compared with, say, deforestation, has historically affected the best quality land. The impact of human settlement on bioproductivity is thus out of proportion to the land take.

The finite nature of land has inevitably also led to conflicts over its use. Many commentators have argued that as we approach ecological limits to growth we will see more widespread examples of such tensions.[24] This was recognized in the report of the UN Secretary General, prepared for the second Earth Summit in 1997,[25] where he stated that 'land-use conflicts between agriculture, forest cover and urban uses are sharpening'.[26]

Such 'sharpenings' are informative and educational to any analysis of land availability. Three key topics are considered below:

- Limits to cropland
- The threats to forests
- Declining biodiversity.

A Hunger for Land

> *'Mosquitoes are the fattest inhabitants of this republic'* (Fred D'Aguiar, Guyanese writer).

Despite a period of unprecedented growth in expenditure on private and public consumption, from an estimated US$1.5 trillion in 1900 to $24 trillion in 1998,[27] we are still unable to adequately feed around 840 million people – about one in seven – of the world's mouths.[28] After falling steadily in the early 1990s, the number of under-nourished people recently showed a slight increase.[29] This hungry 15 per cent of the global population are not suffering as a result of their own inaction or even, necessarily, as a result of an inability to contribute to costs.[30] In many cases they are the victims of a complex set of environmental, social and economic circumstances beyond their control.[31] Access to land for local consumption is an important component (see Box 3.1), for without sufficient land and the means with which to farm it sustainably, there can be no long-term food security.

Are we approaching the limits of available cropland? Some writers think so. In 1993 Stanford University ecologists Paul Ehrlich, Ann Ehrlich and Gretchen Daily commented that most of the world's suitable land was already under cultivation.[32] This was echoed more recently in the 1998–99 World Resources report:

> *'...most high quality agricultural land is already in production, and the environmental costs of converting remaining forest, grassland and wetland habitats to cropland are well recognized. Even if such lands were converted to agricultural uses, much of the remaining soil is less productive and more fragile; thus its contribution to future world food production would likely be limited'.*[33]

The International Food Policy Research Institute (IFPRI) at least partly agrees. It estimates that cropland could, theoretically, be doubled but acknowledges that there are potential problems due to competition for land and difficulties with irrigation. The institute states that 'because of

---

Box 3.1 Rural Poverty

In rural areas, the most crucial asset is land. Gross inequality in land owner-ship is a major obstacle in many countries to improved human security and to agricultural progress. The concentration of land in the hands of a few also reduces productivity and leads to an inefficient use of resources. When modernization of agriculture takes place in this situation, it frequently results in the further marginalization of poor people, who become landless labourers, or smallholders with insufficient land to meet family needs for food and income.

Concentration of land ownership is most marked in Latin America, where feeble efforts at land reform have left the agrarian structures inher-ited from Spanish and Portuguese colonialism largely intact in many countries. Ownership of land in Brazil is among the most concentrated in the world. Nearly eleven million Brazilians who work the land are either landless, or have holdings which are too small to support a family. The poorest one-third of rural families own less than 1 per cent of arable land. At the other end of the scale are the giant *latifundia*: with an average size in excess of 1000 ha, these estates control over 50 per cent of the country's farmland. These big estates account for the bulk of the soya bean, fruit and vegetable exports which make Brazil the fourth-largest agricultural exporter, and one of the main suppliers of high-protein foodstuffs for European beef farmers. The social structure of rural Brazil is better equipped to feed Northern consumers and European cattle than to provide for Brazilians.

Source: Oxfam Poverty Report, Kevin Watkins, Oxfam 1995

---

constraints on the expansion of land and water resources, growth in future food supply depends predominantly on growth in yields'.[34]

Attempts to expand cropland in the past tell a salutary tale. Kazakhstan, the largest wheat producer in Central Asia, has lost one-third of its 26 million ha of cropland to soil erosion following expansion in the 1950s. Saudi Arabia similarly tried to increase grain production in an effort to become self-sufficient. This time failure came about because of the unsustainable use of non-replenishable ground-water reserves. Starved of adequate irrigation, the cropland reverted to desert.[35] In the US water resource problems result from the dramatic lowering of the water table in the grape-growing regions of Southern California and from extractions from the Colorado River, which have created much legal wrangling.[36]

Cropland is also under threat from creeping development. Losses occur as a result of residential development, industrial expansion and the increase in land-intensive leisure facilities such as golf courses.[37] Other impacts, such as the effects of long-term pesticide use and global climate change on land productivity, are more difficult to predict but have nonetheless been highlighted as serious concerns by many environmentalists.[38] Trends would suggest that the problems caused by global climate change are likely to worsen. The year 1998 was particularly bad for weather damage, costing insurers US$90 billion, the second highest figure ever.[39]

Whatever the future of food production, two things remain clear. Firstly, care will have to be taken to protect our existing croplands both from loss of fertility and further encroachment. Secondly, there will be increasing pressure to extend croplands into sensitive habitats, especially in regions where populations are increasing.

Globally, we are going to have to learn to grow more from less. Per capita grain-growing area has decreased from almost 0.23 ha per person in 1950 to 0.12 ha in 1997.[40] If this trend continues, as it is predicted to do, then there will be just 0.08 ha per person in the year 2030.[41]

Papering over the Cracks – the Threat to Forests

'Forests precede civilizations, deserts follow them' (Vicomte de Chateaubriand, French diplomat and writer)

The quality and quantity of the global forest has declined significantly in recent years. Less than half of the planet's original forest cover remains.[42] Of this dwindling area only one-fifth is now categorized as large, relatively undisturbed 'frontier forest'.[43] The situation may be even worse than this, with organizations such as the FAO expressing concerns as to the accuracy of such land use data.

Forest and woodland cover is currently declining at approximately 11 to 15 million ha each year – roughly the equivalent land area to a country the size of Greece or Honduras.[44,45]

What is causing this deforestation? The 1997 *State of the World's Forests* (FAO, Rome) explains that:

> *'Deforestation in tropical regions has continued over the period 1990–95. Recently released information on the causes of deforestation over the 1980–90 decade clearly shows rural population growth coupled with agricultural expansion (especially in Africa and Asia) and economic development programmes (in Latin America and Asia) as major causes of changes in forest cover.'*

In other words, populations make heavy demands on forest lands – for paper, fuelwood and building materials. The most dramatic forest loss occurs where land is transformed into pasture.

The increases in demand for wood products have not always been managed to make best use of this potentially renewable resource, although the situation has certainly improved in recent years.[46]

Nonetheless, examples of unsustainable timber use abound, with Côte d'Ivoire, Nigeria, Philippines and Thailand among some of the major timber exporters that found that they could no longer sustain production.[47] High levels of logging in North America, Canada and Siberia are currently causing concern: Canada, for example, is losing 200,000 ha of forest a year.

In sub-Saharan Africa and Latin America, in particular, the conversion of land to food production is predicted to be a leading cause of deforestation.[48] As the FAO gloomily predict, 'the questions are not whether forest land will be converted to agricultural land, but rather, what forest land will be converted and will such land provide greater benefits being managed for agricultural production than for forest goods and services?'[49]

One often ignored impact of timber harvesting is the building of access roads. As much as one-fifth of a logged forest may be turned over to carriageway.[50] This leads to forest fragmentation, increasing the incidence of invasive species and encouraging further use of the land for leisure and settlement, potentially hindering regeneration.

The loss of forest cover has many environmental consequences. Deforestation and overexploitation of forests are major causes of soil degradation in dry areas.[51] Forests are important in the control of erosion, soil stabilization and water regulation, particularly in mountainous regions. They provide a home for an estimated two-thirds of the species on the planet and play a key role in regulating our climate. The latter point requires some further expansion as it relates directly to the role of forest land in ecological footprint analysis.

The main 'greenhouse gas' implicated in global climate change is carbon dioxide (CO_2). About three-quarters of the human-related CO_2 released into the atmosphere is a result of fossil-fuel burning, with changing land use accounting for most of the remainder. The effects of human activity add approximately three billion tonnes of carbon per year to the atmosphere.[52]

Terrestrial vegetation plays an important role in the regulation of the carbon cycle. The burning and decay of forests leads to a release of carbon just as new forest growth can absorb, or sequester, carbon from the atmosphere. For this reason, reducing deforestation and promoting reafforestation has been seen by many policy-makers as a means of offsetting carbon emissions from fossil-fuel use. Studies show, however, that this strategy in itself is not sufficient to deal with the historical and projected levels of emissions (see Box 3.2).[53,54,]

It is clear, however, that land is set to become humanity's most limiting resource. The surface of our planet is finite, a tailor-made world with the limitation that one size must fit all. If we outgrow this earth there are no other places we can go.

Box 3.2 Forests as Carbon Sinks

The vegetation and soils of the world's forests contain a vast quantity of carbon – more than one-and-a-quarter times the amount stored in the atmosphere. CO_2 is released when forests are cleared or degraded, and vegetation is burned or decays. Burning forest vegetation also releases other greenhouse gases, including methane (CH_4), nitrous oxide (N_2O), carbon monoxide (CO), and oxides of nitrogen (NO_x).

When forests grow, CO_2 is withdrawn from the atmosphere through photosynthesis and stored as carbon in the vegetation. Levels of carbon in the soil may be increased by reafforestation and other forest management practices. Currently, the world's forests are estimated to be net sources of CO_2, primarily due to deforestation and forest degradation in the tropics. Temperate and boreal forests, which overall are slightly increasing in area and in some places in biomass per unit area, are net carbon sinks. The following three forest-related strategies have been proposed as means to influence CO_2 emissions:

1 maintaining existing carbon stocks through forest management and conservation;
2 increasing storage of carbon in forests (by increasing forest area or biomass per unit area) and in forest products; and
3 substituting fossil fuels with fuelwood from sustainably managed forests, and substituting energy-expensive products (for example, steel, aluminium, concrete) with industrial wood products.

The third strategy, termed 'substitution management', has the greatest long-term potential for greenhouse gas mitigation. Unlike the first two, which can produce only finite increases in terrestrial carbon storage, this third group of activities can reduce net CO_2 emissions indefinitely. Emissions from fossil fuels are avoided, and emissions from wood are balanced by subsequent regrowth.

The IPCC estimates that about 12–15 per cent of the projected CO_2 emissions from fossil fuel consumption from now until 2050 could be offset by slowing deforestation, promoting forest regeneration, and increasing the area in plantations and other managaged forestry systems. Tropical forests have the greatest potential for sequestering carbon; they could provide 80 per cent of increased storage of carbon in the world's forests, mainly through forest regeneration and reduced deforestation. Tropical America has the greatest potential for increasing carbon storage, followed by Asia and then tropical Africa.

Source: FAO (1997) *State of the World's Forests*, FAO, Rome

*describes rates of
decrease. +
how we're the
source of it.*

Suffering in Silence – Declining Diversity

> *'Until lions have their historians, tales of hunting will always glorify the hunter'* (African saying)

As is apparent from the previous section, one of the main victims of deforestation is biological diversity. Forests are home to an estimated two-thirds of the world's species. The richest forest habitats are undoubtedly the tropical rainforests, which cover about 7 per cent of the land mass of the earth. Other species-rich habitats include the coral reefs and wetlands, each in decline. For example, US wetlands have declined in size by 95 per cent since 1800.

Studies estimate an annual species loss of at least 1000 times the 'natural' background rate, equivalent to around one plant species and many more animal species per day (a range of 10 to 100 per day is often quoted).[55] We are in the midst of what some environmentalists have termed a 'mass extinction' caused by human activity.[56,57]

The percentage of species at risk of extinction varies by region partly as a function of the natural diversity and partly due to the level of harmful human intervention. A recent report by the World Wide Fund For Nature (WWF)[58] shows Mauritius to be the worst hit country with almost 40 per cent of bird and mammal species threatened, followed by New Zealand (29 per cent) and Madagascar (20 per cent).

There is a large degree of uncertainty about the rate of decline as we still know surprisingly little about the other organisms that share this planet. To date around 1.8 million species have been identified of which less than 16,000 are mammals and birds,[59] yet this is recognized to be just the tip of the biodiversity iceberg. Anywhere up to 40 million other organisms have yet to be catalogued.[60] Many are likely to be declining or in serious decline without our knowledge.

Birds are probably the most studied of all creatures, with almost 10,000 known species. They are also a good general indicator of the health of wildlife as they tend to be at, or near, the top of the food chain. In the UK, for example, it has been proposed by the government that bird numbers should be used as a proxy for rural environmental quality.[61]

Historical data show that farmland and woodland have generally been declining since the mid-1970s. The authoritative information source on endangered animals is the World Conservation Union 'Red Book' which is published annually. Data from 1996 show that 39 per cent of mammals and fish, 30 per cent of amphibians, 26 per cent of reptiles and 20 per cent of bird species are in danger of, or under threat of, extinction.

The main reason for species decline is, not surprisingly, habitat loss.[62] At the second Earth Summit it was stated: 'The threat to biodiversity stems mainly from habitat destruction, overharvesting,

---

Box 3.3 Status of the Tiger

There are no recent accurate estimates of the world tiger population. Their numbers have declined dramatically by about 95 per cent since the turn of the century – from perhaps 100,000 to 5000. In the past 60 years, three subspecies have become extinct. The Bali tiger became extinct in the 1940s; the Caspian tiger in the 1970s and the Javan tiger in the 1980s. The South China tiger is now on the verge of extinction with just 30 individuals estimated to be alive.

Until the 1930s, hunting for sport was probably the main cause for the decline in tiger populations. Between the 1940s and the late 1980s, the greatest threat was loss of habitat because of activities such as logging or mineral exploitation. Habitat destruction may also have had an indirect influence on tiger populations through a reduction in the availability of prey.

Source: WWF (http://www.panda.org last accessed 30 November 1999)

---

pollution and the inappropriate introduction of foreign plants and animals'.

The land use tensions are all too familiar: agriculture, livestock grazing, logging, leisure uses and urbanization. Many species are adapted to very specific ecological conditions and can be wiped out by disruption within a relatively small geographical area. Well-documented examples include the loss of two-thirds of Hawaii's unique bird species and the decline in the number of tiger species worldwide (see Box 3.3).[63]

It would be wrong to consider deteriorating natural habitats only in terms of forests or other wild lands. In fact, aquatic ecosystems contain possibly the largest proportion of species in immediate danger of extinction. Thirteen per cent of surveyed fish species are so classified with a further 21 per cent considered as 'vulnerable to extinction', suggesting that a third of all fish species may be close to disappearing.[64,65] Fish are the most diverse group of vertebrates, occupying a great range of aquatic habitats from Lake Titicaca, the highest body of fresh water, to Lake Baikal, the deepest, as well as the world's vast oceans.

Although the types of environment may be different from those of land-based species, the reasons for decline are all too familiar. Habitat loss particularly affects inland environments. It is estimated that at least 60 per cent of freshwater species are in decline as a result of habitat alteration.[66] The insatiable demand for fresh water has led to increasing human intervention in hydrological systems – rivers are dammed or drained dry, basins are flooded, waterways canalized and flood plains built upon.

But pelagic species, those that inhabit the open seas, are faring little better. Overfishing and pollution have resulted in steadily declining catches and depleted stocks in all of the world's fishing regions, to the point where some commercial species such as the Atlantic cod, bluefin tuna and haddock have been added to the Red Book list of endangered species. This has significant implications for feeding the global population, who get 5 per cent of their overall protein intake, amounting to 20 per cent of animal protein, from seafood.[67] This, however, masks considerable regional variations in diet, with around one billion people relying on seafood as their primary source of protein.[68]

A response to the decline in ocean fish stocks has been to rapidly increase fish farming – in the last 20 years aquaculture has grown steadily to provide more than 15 per cent of our fish products.[69] Of course, such intensive farming not only uses space but requires an input of feed, primarily grain, and energy.

As elsewhere, we are shoring up our failing renewable resources by thinly spreading what resources we still have, resorting to more non-renewable, energy-intensive production methods. We cannot postpone the ecological realities of living within a finite world for much longer. We are not only shuffling the deckchairs on a sinking planetary *Titanic*, but trying to convert the hull into further seating!

CARRYING CAPACITY

The thinking behind ecological footprint analysis builds on the concept of carrying capacity – the ability of the earth to support life.

Carrying capacity is a term used by biologists to describe the number of animals of a given species that a defined habitat can support indefinitely. For example, farmers must know how many cows can be grazed on their pastures or wildlife biologists will want to know the number of deer that can be supported by a certain sized forest.

For many years the concept evaded application to human beings. Some argued that humans, unlike cows and deer, are able to adapt their environment and thus increase its carrying capacity. This is certainly the case. For example, before the advent of settled agriculture it has been estimated that a single hunter-gatherer would have had to forage more than 100 ha of tropical rainforest. Today, intensive farming methods have increased yields to the extent that the equivalent area of arable land could potentially feed around 1000 people per year, albeit at a very basic subsistence level and on a restricted diet.[70]

Yet if we accept that there are natural constraints on the regenerative capacity of the planet – and the evidence is that we seem to be reaching or exceeding such limits at a time of rising population[71] – then the urgent questions that need to be asked are:

- How far can we increase the productivity of our natural systems to cope with increased consumption and population?

Box 3.4 Overshoot – Sustainability's Big Taboo

Our dominant culture continues to celebrate expansion in spite of its heavy toll on people and nature. In fact, we desperately try to ignore that much of today's income stems from liquidating our social and natural assets. We fool ourselves into believing that we can disregard ecological limits indefinitely. We actively resist the idea that there are biophysical limits and shield ourselves with wealth from the fallout of ecological overshoot. Limits are seen as taboo. Instead of engaging people, it seems talking about limits threatens them. Nevertheless, limits exist, are at the core of the sustainability dilemma, and put additional pressure on social equity.

In a recent interview, Nafis Sadik, executive director of the UN Population Fund, stated that 'many environmentalists think [that the carrying capacity of the earth] is four billion, maximum. But now we have six billion people'.[72]

This is not the contradiction it first seems. Ecological limits can be exceeded for some time because nature reacts with some inertia. More precisely, natural capital can be harvested faster than it regenerates, thereby depleting the capital stock. Ecologists have observed this 'overshoot dynamics' with many species – and human civilizations.

Indeed, it is possible that human consumption is waxing, as pointed out by economist Julian Simon, while ecological capacity is waning, as pointed out by environmentalist Norman Myers.[73] Overshoot explains why these two story lines are not necessarily contradictory, but two sides of the same coin.

This is why systematic resource accounting is so fundamental to sustainability. As long as our governments and business leaders do not know how much nature we use as compared to how much nature there is, overshoot may go undetected – derailing society further and further away from sustainability.

- Can we produce more without further limiting the ability of future generations to provide for themselves?
- How is this intervention impacting on other species?

Once it is accepted that carrying-capacity principles are applicable to humanity, then we must acknowledge that many of the features of population growth and decay, previously observed in other animal species, could – under certain circumstances – equally well apply to people.

One of the more uncomfortable principles to accept is that of overshoot (see Box 3.4 and the 'bad joke' portrayed in Figure 3.2). As with any other species, it is feasible, and indeed possible, that humanity is overshooting the carrying capacity of its environment, thereby depleting nature's productive capacity.

Such overshoot can have dramatic consequences, as for example in the sad tale of population growth, overshoot and crash on Easter Island (Box 3.5).

Figure 3.2 *Declaring that current levels of consumption can be maintained, on the basis that we are already consuming at this rate, reminds the authors of the warped logic of a bad joke. It is like the stuntman who, jumping from the top of a 50-storey building, declares to onlookers as he passes the fifth floor that his stunt is a perfect success because, so far, he has not been hurt*

A GROWING GLOBAL FAMILY

> *'Land belongs to one large family, few of whom are alive, many of whom are dead, countless of whom are yet unborn'* (Dr R S Mogoba on African land tenure, 1992)

If you want to know how many people there are on the planet, visit the population clock on the US census bureau web site.[74] If you pause a minute to grab a cup of coffee on the way, another 150 people will have been added to the global population, equal to around 80 million each year.[75] To think of it another way, that is more than the population of London, New York, Mexico City, Beijing, Cairo and Bombay combined.

According to the UN, the global population officially passed the symbolic six billion mark on 12 October 1999. No one quite knows the

---

Box 3.5 The Easter Island Story

When Easter Island was first settled a thousand years ago, the island was a rich and forested land covered with palms and a small native tree called the sophora. On its 64 square miles (16,500 ha) a prosperous and literate culture developed with organizational and engineering skills that enabled it to erect the famous, massive stone statues all along the coastline. The population of the island over the years increased to something like 4000 people, apparently necessitating a steady 'drawdown' of vegetation that eventually resulted in deforestation of the entire island and the exhaustion of its fertile soils. Somewhere along the line came overshoot – unstoppable and final – and then a population crash which was presumably hastened by conflict over scarce food, leading ultimately to warfare and chaos. By the time of Captain Cook's voyage to the island in 1775 there were barely 630 people left, eking out a marginal existence; 100 years later, only 155 islanders remained.

---

real population figure. It has even been argued that six billion was reached in late 1997 – a not unreasonable suggestion, requiring an under-recording of only 2 per cent.[76]

The maximum carrying capacity of 'spaceship earth' has taxed many minds in the last 200 years. In 1790 the British economist Reverend Thomas Malthus wrote in his *Essay on the Principle of Population* that:

> *'It is an obvious truth, which has been taken notice of by many writers, that population must always be kept down to the level of the means of subsistence; but no writer that the Author recollects has inquired particularly into the means by which this level is effected: and it is a view of these means which forms, to his mind, the strongest obstacle in the way to any very great future improvement of society.[77]*

He went on to argue that whereas population growth is likely to be exponential (it rises at a relatively constant growth rate), any productivity increases in land are inevitably going to be less rapid. This, he predicted, would result in a 'perpetual struggle for room and food'.

Later writers highlighted the role played by consumption patterns, technology and the global market place in undermining Malthus' basic arguments.[78] Human ingenuity has ensured that our demands on the environment have consistently been met – or so it would seem at first glance – but at what cost to future generations?

Perhaps the fullest analysis of the literature on global carrying capacity is that of Joel E Cohen.[79] Taking the data contained within Cohen's comprehensive review, the authors have plotted the various historical estimates of carrying capacity alongside population (see

Box 3.6 How Many People can the Earth Support? A Critical Review

Joel E Cohen must be congratulated for tackling this most basic carrying-capacity question. Unfortunately, he does not come up with a satisfying answer.

By avoiding an analysis of human 'load' and ecological limits, Cohen has dispensed with a large body of helpful literature such as the work of Peter Vitousek (1986), William Catton (1980) and others. In the authors' view it is the very fact that ecological capacity can be used beyond its sustainable limits that makes present consumption levels of most concern (Wackernagel et al, 1999). Failing to acknowledge the possibility of overshoot in turn denies the possibility of population collapse (Dobkowski and Walliman, 1999)

With respect to some of the more extreme estimates of carrying capacity reported by Cohen, the use of simple quantitative analysis can help to tease out the more ridiculous suggestions. Consider, for example, the 1000 billion maximum supportable population attributed to Marchetti (1978). Such a figure can easily be refuted by applying some common-sense 'back-of-the-envelope' calculations using FAO data.

If we generously assume that the ecologically productive area remains as now – around 10.3 billion ha – this translates to 100 m^2 (or 0.01 ha) per capita, allowing for 3 m^2 of living space. Currently, one hectare of world average arable land can produce about 2800 kg of cereals per year (let us ignore that these yields are only possible with high levels of fertilizer application). In addition, arable land is the most fertile land category and turns out to be roughly three times more productive than average bioproductive land. In other words, the 100 m^2 of such average land available per person corresponds to a yearly harvest of about 10 kg of cereals.[80]

Each kilogram of cereals contains 13,000 kilojoules of nutritional energy, or 30 per cent more than the daily calorific requirement of an average person. Assuming direct use and no losses from farm to mouth, a population of 1000 billion would be guaranteed a subsistence diet for just 13 days a year. They would, of course, also have to go without timber to build, energy to heat (apart from a small amount of straw per person), fibres to clothe, space to protect other species, or any other ecological function which needs land area.

Further information can be found in the following sources: Cohen, 1995,[81] Catton, 1980,[82] Dobkowski and Walliman, 1998,[83] Vitousek, Ehrlich, Ehrlich and Mateson, 1986,[84] Wackernagel et al, 1999[85]

Figure 3.3). A wide range of upper limits has been suggested – from as low as one billion to as high as 1,000,000,000 (10^9) billion. As Cohen himself points out, some of the higher estimates are based on somewhat unrealistic assumptions, or written with a certain element of dry humour (see Box 3.6). To put these estimates into perspective, two-thirds of the estimates suggest a maximum limit of less than 15 billion.

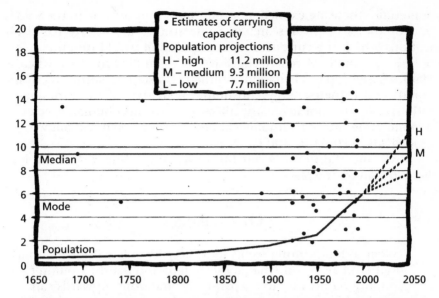

Figure 3.3 *Historical estimates of global carrying capacity set against population growth; median estimate is 9.5 billion; modal estimate is 5.5 billion*

Revisiting the data collated by Cohen, the authors have plotted 63 historical estimates of global carrying capacity by the year of estimate against historical and projected population growth (see Figure 3.3). To this, horizontal lines representing the median and modal estimates of maximum supportable populations have been added. Seen against the population trends, these give pause for thought – the authors have labelled the region between the mode and median estimates as a 'warning zone'.

In the mid-1980s the global population crossed into this 'warning zone' – exceeding the most frequently stated maximum supportable number and, based on the UN medium projections, will pass the median line (the 'middle' estimate) some time soon after 2050.[86]

All estimates of global capacity should come with a strongly worded 'health warning'. There are many factors to consider when deriving such limits. Cohen concludes that 'to make more credible estimates of human carrying capacity, scientists must learn more of the four-way interactions of population, the environment, economy and culture.'[87]

Cohen suggests that we first need to answer questions such as 'what do people want to eat?', 'what expectations do they have for their health?', 'where do people want to live?', and 'how do we want to treat non-human species?' Indeed it can be argued that it makes no sense to talk about global carrying capacity at all without defining your terms.

Estimates of carrying capacity vary not just because of calculation differences, but because of the range of differing assumptions made.

Sometimes these are explicit, at other times they are due to the values and opinions of the researcher. Some studies are clearly based on notions which the current human population would find unacceptable. For example, Marchetti suggested living in floating cities, whereas Hardin based some calculations on the premise that North Americans could reduce their energy consumption to that of the Ethiopians. Others still have not made any allowances for non-human species or assume some future technological breakthrough that will allow high crop yields in currently arid lands.[88]

Such uncertainties cry out for a unifying framework to explore human load on the planet.

QUESTIONS

- Ecological footprinting seems to be very 'two dimensional'. It talks about land areas but what about height and depth? Couldn't our economy continue to expand by building upwards and/or downwards? (see Chapter 6, Question 7)
- Why do you give so much attention to renewable resources? Aren't they sustainable already? (see Chapter 6, Question 13)
- Ecological footprinting implies that trade is bad. How are highly populous countries or communities meant to survive? (see Chapter 6, Question 16).

NOTES

1   In 1990 Mathis Wackernagel developed the idea in his doctoral thesis under Professor William Rees at the University of British Columbia, Canada. Originally they referred to the concept as 'appropriated carrying capacity'. Soon Bill Rees came up with a better name – the 'ecological footprint'. This term was, in turn, picked up from a computer delivery man who bragged that Bill's new machine would certainly have a smaller footprint on Bill's desk than his previous one. The term is now so commonly used that it appears in the new *Oxford English Dictionary*.

2   List adapted from Young, A, 1998, *Land Resources: Now and for the future*, p50, Cambridge University Press

3   Included in this category are air photography, geographical information systems (GIS) and digital image processing. However, the authors recognize that remote sensing techniques have their limitations. They cannot talk to local people, take soil samples or substitute for the trained eye of a local farmer

4   The authors' land estimates vary from those given in *World Resources 1998–1999*, Oxford University Press, as we include areas such as Antarctica. Figures for forest and woodland are also higher as we include lightly wooded areas (those with less than 10 per cent of tree cover)

5   See their web site www.fao.org (last visited 29/11/99) for the most up-to-date figures. These land use data are also published in the annual World

Resources series. See, for example, World Resources Institute, *World Resources 1998–1999, A guide to the global environment*, Oxford: Oxford University Press

6   It should be noted that there is some degree of disagreement between the various data sources

7   Sources: World Resources Institute, *World Resources 1998–1999*, Oxford, Oxford University Press; FAO website www.fao.org, January 1998; Wackernagel and Rees, 1996, *Our Ecological Footprint*, New Society, Canada; Bakkes, J A and J W van Woerden (eds), 1997, *The Future of the Global Environment*, RIVM/UNEP, a model-based analysis supporting UNEP's first Global Environment Outlook, RIVM 402001007 and UNEP/DEIA/TR 97–1; Costanza et al, 'The Value of the World's Ecosystem Services and Natural Capital', *Nature*, vol 387, pp253–260; *State of the World's Forests 1997*, FAO

8   World Resources Institute 1999, *World Resources 1998–1999, A guide to the global environment*, Oxford University Press

9   Comments to this effect in *World Resources 1998–99*, p302, Oxford, Oxford University Press

10   Forest data calculated by Wackernagel based on information contained within *State of the World's Forests 1995*, FAO, 1995

11   Young, A, 1998, *Land Resources: Now and for the Future*, Cambridge University Press, estimates that 4300 Mha are deserts, mountains, rock outcrops or ice-covered

12   Estimates tend to be based on calculations of urban population densities. The reporting of built land is particularly sensitive and can vary depending on the assumptions made and definitions used

13   Bakkes, J A and J W van Woerden (eds), 1997, *The Future of the Global Environment: A model-based analysis supporting UNEP's first Global Environment Outlook*, RIVM/UNEP: RIVM 402001007 and UNEP/DEIA/TR 97-1, pp78/79. World Resources provide a figure for domesticated land (based on modification for agricultural use only) of 37 per cent. The authors' figures are lower because our global land figure is higher

14   Estimates include 8.9 billion hectares (Wackernagel and Rees, 1996, op cit), 8.7 billion hectares (Young, A, 1998). More recent estimates by Wackernagel include lightly wooded areas (based on data from FAO, 1997, *State of the World's Forests*) pushing the area classified as productive to almost 10 billion hectares. If one also includes built land, which in most cases was formerly productive, then the total is 10.3 hectares

15   This term covers Australia, Fiji, New Zealand, Solomon Islands, Papua New Guinea

16   Interest in the appropriation of 'distant elsewheres' dates back at least a hundred years. The mainly agricultural economies of the Mediterranean basin, for example, were based around the trading of foodstuffs. See, for example, Fernand Braudel's 'Le Méditerranée' – first written in 1949 – a chronicle of the Mediterranean in the late 16th century ('La Méditerranée et le monde méditerranéen à l'époque de Philippe II 2 éd', 1966, Paris: Armand Colin). Other examples include William Stanley Jevons' 'The coal question: an inquiry concerning the progress of the nation, and the probable exhaustion of our coal-mines, 3rd edition', 1906, London, Macmillan, and, more recently, the work of Georg Borgstrom on 'ghost acreages' (see *Harvesting the Earth*, NY, Abelard-Schuman, 1973)

17   Data from EuroStat for 1993 (Source: *Europe in Figures: 4th Edition*) show
      a positive trade balance in agricultural goods of more than 10 billion
      ECUs whereas the Friends of the Earth land calculations for the same
      period show a net import of around 12 million hectares (Friends of the
      Earth Europe, 1995, *Towards Sustainable Europe*)
18   See 'Who lives in the "global village"?'
      http://www.empowermentresources.com/info2/theglobalvillage.html,
      last accessed 31/3/00
19   The spreadsheet 'Global Village II' can be downloaded from
      http://www.ecologicalfootprint.com
20   Postel, S, 1994, 'Carrying Capacity: Earth's Bottom Line', in *The State of
      the World 1994*, p10, Earthscan
21   WRI, UNEP, UNDP, World Bank, 1998, *World Resources 98–99*,
      pp156–157, Oxford University Press
22   UNEP, 1999, *Global Environment Outlook 2000*, p36, Earthscan
23   WRI, UNEP, UNDP, World Bank, 1998, op cit
24   For example, see the annual State of the World reports published by
      Earthscan. Most include topics that relate directly to land use conflicts
      and limits
25   Variously known as Earth Summit II, Rio +5, the United Nations General
      Assembly Special Session (UNGASS) or the 19th Special Session of the
      General Assembly to review progress achieved in the implementation of
      Agenda 21, the event occurred in New York in June 1997
26   Report reproduced in D Osborn and T Bigg, *Earth Summit II: Outcomes
      and Analysis*, 1998, Earthscan, p101
27   Consumption expenditure and malnutrition figures from UNDP, *Human
      Development Report 1998*, pp1 and 48
28   Many more than this are not adequately fed. The number given includes
      only those not able to meet their basic calorific needs
29   News Release from FAO, 26th November 1998
      http://www.fao.org/NEWS/1998
30   The UNDP *Human Development Report 1998* debunked a series of myths
      about the reliance of the poor on subsidies and hand-outs (p84), op cit
31   See UNDP, 1998, p88 'The way forward: food and health care'
32   Ehrlich, P R, Ehrlich, A H and Daily, G C, 1993, *Population & Development
      Review* vol 19, no 1, pp1–32
33   WRI, UNEP, UNDP, World Bank, 1998, *World Resources 98–99*, pp152
      Oxford University Press
34   Conclusions from a Round Table on Food and Population to 2010,
      Nurul Islam (ed) International Food Policy Research Institute (IFPRI)
      2020 Initiative, http://www.cgiar.org/ifpri/2020/synth/islam.htm
35   Brown, L, Flavin, C, and French, H, 1998, *State of the World 1998* – 'The
      Future of Growth', p6, Earthscan
36   *Los Angeles Times*, August 29th 1998, 'Legislators Try to Save Water Deal'
37   Brown, L, Flavin, C, and French, H, 1998, *State of the World 1998*,
      'Struggling to raise Cropland Productivity', p80, Earthscan
38   Brown, L, Flavin, C, and French, H, 1998, *State of the World 1998*, 'The
      Future of Growth', p10, Earthscan
39   *Daily Telegraph*, 30th December 1998
40   Grain is often used as a proxy for cropland productivity as it is the
      largest category of produce and the most fully documented

41   Brown, L, Flavin, C, and French, H, 1998, *State of the World 1998*
     'Struggling to raise Cropland Productivity', p81, Earthscan
42   WRI, UNEP, UNDP, World Bank, 1998, *World Resources 98–99*, p294,
     Oxford University Press
43   WRI, UNEP, UNDP, World Bank, 1998, *World Resources 98-99*, pp294–5
     Oxford University Press.
44   Calculated from average annual change between 1990 and 1995 total
     forest extent figures in *World Resources 98–99*, p292. The figure is proba-
     bly closer to 11 million hectares. Greece has an area of 12.9 million
     hectares, Honduras has an area of 11.2 million hectares
45   Higher estimate of 15 million hectares per annum from *State of the
     World's Forests 1997*, FAO, p12
46   Ibid, p33
47   Brown, L, Flavin, C, and French, H, 1998, *State of the World 1998*, 'The
     Future of Growth', Earthscan, London, p9
48   Figures on forest cover and information on regional variations are based
     on the information contained in the comprehensive *State of the World's
     Forests 1997* (FAO, 1997) report except where indicated (pp18–22)
49   FAO, 1997, *State of the World's Forests 1997*, p43
50   Brown, L, Flavin, C, and French, H, 1998, *State of the World 1998*,
     'Sustaining the World's Forests', p25. Calculated from the figures given
     assuming a conservative carriageway width and verge of 10 metres
51   FAO, 1997, *State of the World's Forests 1997*, p39
52   See, for example, Winjum, J K, Dixon, R K and Schroeder, P E, 1992,
     Estimating the Global Potential of Forest and Agroforest Management
     Practices to Sequester Carbon, *Water, Soil and Air Pollution*, vol 64,
     pp213–227; Krause, F, Bach, W and Koomey, J, 1990, *Energy Policy in the
     Greenhouse*, pp13–28, Earthscan
53   It has been argued that the ocean already sequesters up to 40 per cent of
     carbon emissions from fossil fuels (for example, see the work of Ben
     Matthews of the University of East Anglia and Global Commons
     Institute; website: http://www.cgi.org). Due to uncertainty about the
     future stability of oceanic sinks, the authors prefer to treat all sequestra-
     tion as land-based using conservative absorption factors
54   See also Krause, Bach and Koomey, 1990, *Energy Policy in the Greenhouse*,
     Earthscan; Mattoon, A T, 1998, 'Bogging down in the Sinks',
     Worldwatch, see http://www.worldwatch.org
55   Meadows, D H, Meadows, D L, and Randers, J, 1992, *Beyond the Limits*,
     p65, Earthscan
56   Brown, L, Flavin, C, and French, H, 1998, *State of the World 1998*, p41
57   Myers, N, *The Gaia Atlas of Future Worlds*, p34, Robertson McCarta
58   'Living Planet Report', 1998, WWF
     http://www.panda.org/livingplanet/pubs.html. The 'Living Planet Report
     2000' uses ecological footprinting
59   *World Resources 98–99*, p322
60   State *of the World 1998*, p42
61   'Sustainability Counts', UK Department of the Environment, Transport
     and the Regions, 1999
62   *State of the World 1998*, p44. Numerous other examples are cited by E O
     Wilson in *The Diversity of Life*, Belknap Press of Harvard University Press,
     1992 (UK edition Allen Lane, The Penguin Press, 1993)

63   *State of the World 1998*, p45
64   *State of the World 1998*, p52
65   *World Resource 98-99*, p190
66   *State of the World 1998*, p53
67   FAO data for 1996 from FAO website http://www.fao.org
68   *World Resources 98-99*, p196
69   FAO data from web site http://www.fao.org
70   Calculation based on a usable yield of 2 tonnes of grain per hectare and a grain-only diet of 200kg annual consumption (the bare minimum to meet food energy needs). In contrast the average European consumes more than double this amount of grain, both directly and indirectly, as part of a more varied diet of meat and vegetables. Data on carrying capacity for hunter-gatherer from T R E Southwood in *Monitoring the Environment*, edited by Bryan Cartledge, 1992, OUP. It should be pointed out that comparing yields of unmanaged natural forest and intensively-farmed arable land is not an entirely fair comparison. The indirect effects of farming have not been taken into account, nor have the biodiversity impacts or any differences in basic land bioproductivity
71   See, for example, *Global Environment Outlook (GEO) 2000*, United Nations Environment Programme (UNEP), Earthscan, London, 1999
72   See Jim Motavalli, 1999, 'Conversations with Dr Nafis Sadik: The UN's Prescription for Family Planning', *The Environmental Magazine*, July/August 1999, vol 10, no 4, pp10–13
73   Norman Myers, and Julian L Simon, 1994, *Scarcity or Abundance? A Debate on the Environment*, Norton, New York/London
74   http://www.census.gov/cgi-bin/ipc/popclockw or try http://www.worldgame.org
75   *World Resources 1998–99*, p141
76   Proposed by Anthony Young, author of *Land Resources: Now and for the Future*, Cambridge University Press, Cambridge 1998. See his website: http://www.land-resource.org
77   Malthus' full essay is available on the internet and website: http://socsci.mcmaster.ca/~econ/ugcm/3113/malthus/popu.txt (accessed on 23rd October 1999)
78   For a more detailed analysis of Malthus' arguments see Cohen, 1995
79   Joel E Cohen, 1995, *How Many People can the Earth Support?*, 1995, Norton
80   Simply estimated by assuming one-third of average arable productivity is possible using every available hectare of productive land. 100m^2 would yield 2800/3 kg of cereals per year (about 1000 kg)
81   Cohen, Joel E, 1995, op cit
82   Catton, W R Jr, 1980, *Overshoot: The Ecological Basis of Revolutionary Change*, Urbana, University of Illinois Press.
83   Dobkowski, M N and Wallimann, I (eds), 1998, *The Coming Age of Scarcity: preventing mass death and genocide in the twenty-first century*, Syracuse, NY, Syracuse University Press
84   Peter M, Vitousek, Paul R Ehrlich, Ann H Ehrlich and Pamela A Mateson, 1986, 'Human Appropriation of the Products of Photosynthesis' *BioScience*, vol 36, no 6
85   Wackernagel, M, Onisto, L, Bello, P, 1999, 'National Natural Capital Accounting with the Ecological Footprint Concept', *Ecological Economics*, vol 29, no 3, pp375–390

86   It is important to note that the UN projections take no account of resource constraints, thus the possibility of overshoot and population collapse is not considered
87   Op cit, note 85, p386
88   Quoted in Cohen, 1995, op cit, pp413 and 415

Chapter 4

Footprinting Fundamentals

DON'T COUNT THE HEADS – MEASURE THE SIZE OF THE FEET!

'Every human being represents hands to work, and not just another mouth to feed' (George H Bush, former US President, 1991)

Ecological footprint analysis aims to overcome some of the problems of estimating sustainable capacity by turning the key question on its head. Rather than asking 'How many people can the earth support?', footprinting asks 'How much land do people require to support themselves?' In other words, footprinting addresses not the number of heads but the size of the feet.

The question posed is therefore not solely one of human numbers but of population, consumption and technology – which takes us back to the IPAT formula discussed in Chapter 1. In addition, footprinting tries to address biophysical constraints. It does this by comparing our impact on the environment with the capacity of the biosphere to regenerate. The problem can be expressed in terms of human 'load' on the planet – the bioproductive area appropriated by a person (though we later show how footprint analysis can be applied to products, activities, organizations and regions). Catton suggested that an environment's carrying capacity is best defined as its 'maximum persistently supportable load'.[1]

Any analysis of sustainability requires a means of measuring this load. Returning to the old management adage: 'if you can't measure it you can't manage it'. This is equally as relevant to a study of our natural resources as it is to our financial economy.

In many ways, the footprint can be viewed as a form of environmental accounting that respects ecological limits in a way that conventional economics, with its monetary assessment of value, does not. As Inge Røpke has argued, 'Prices are very strange conglomerates that do not have any kind of objective messages to tell about the value of things from either the use side or the cost side'.[2]

ACCOUNTING FOR LAND

Ecological footprint calculations are based on two straightforward assumptions:

1   That we are able to estimate with reasonable accuracy the resources we consume and wastes we generate.
2   That these resource and waste flows can be converted to the equivalent biologically productive area necessary to provide these functions.

Using area equivalence, the ecological footprint aims to express how much of nature's 'interest' we are currently appropriating. If more bioproductive space is required than is available, then we can reasonably state that the rate of consumption is not sustainable. As we shall see, the basic ecological footprinting method provides a conservative estimate of the amount of nature's interest that we are using.

As the ecological footprint analysis (EFA) uses a common currency – bioproductive area – a broad range of impacts can be aggregated to derive footprints for complex activities, objects or regions. The model is additive. The total footprint is determined by adding the individual resource and waste footprints, taking care to avoid any 'double counting' of environmental impacts that could be accommodated within the same bioproductive space.

Consider a cooked meal of lamb and rice. The lamb requires a certain amount of grazing land, road space for transportation, and energy for processing, transportation and cooking. Similarly, the rice requires arable land for production, road space for transportation and energy for processing, transportation and cooking. A detailed ecological footprint analysis would consider all of these environmental impacts, and possibly more, when calculating a total footprint.

Of course, the footprint is not usually a continuous piece of land or land of one particular type or quality. The globalization of trade has increased the likelihood that the bioproductive areas required to support the consumption – of the richer countries at least – are scattered all over the planet. If you were eating the meal suggested above in Europe then it is entirely possible that the lamb would have been reared on New Zealand pastures and the rice grown in Italian fields.

Figure 4.1 *The globalization of trade has meant that items we consume, whether foodstuffs or consumer products, could have travelled half way round the world before reaching us*

LAND TYPES

When undertaking a footprint analysis it is convenient to distinguish between the following categories of ecological space: arable land, pasture land, built or degraded land, forest land and productive sea space. These are chosen because they reflect the categories used by the primary data sources, most notably the FAO. Sometimes it is possible to go into finer detail about land types when, for example, undertaking local projects where more accurate land surveys have been undertaken. The main land categories used for footprinting are defined below.

• Arable land is, biologically speaking, the most productive land. It can grow the largest amount of plant biomass. It is typically used for staple crops such as grains, tubers and pulses.

- Pasture land is used primarily for grazing cattle. Typically, it is less productive than arable land. In addition, conversion efficiencies from plant to animal reduce the available biochemical energy to humans by about a factor of ten (although this depends on the animal produce in question and the management practices used).
- Forested land refers to farmed or natural forests that can yield timber products. Of course, they secure many other functions too, such as erosion prevention, climate stability, maintenance of hydrological cycles, and if they are managed properly, biodiversity protection. For presentation purposes, the authors sometimes combine the forest, pasture and arable lands into a 'productive land' category (see Figure 4.2).
- Productive sea space. Although the vast majority of the earth's surface (over 36 billion ha) is covered by oceans, it is worth remembering that most commercial fishing (somewhere around 90 per cent of the catch) occurs within about 300 km of the shore or in just 8 per cent (2.9 billion ha) of the sea area. This is because the coastal areas are the most productive.[3,4]
- Built land is land where productive capacity has been largely lost by development – roads, buildings and so on. The pattern of human settlement invariably means that the most productive arable land is used for building.
- Energy land is an additional category that the authors use to distinguish the land that would be needed to sustainably manage our

---

Box 4.1 Estimating Land Productivities

Using FAO data it is possible to determine the productivity of different land types by reference to the reported yields of various plant and animal produce.

Arable land is 2.8 times more productive than world average (bioproductive) land. That is, it can produce 280 per cent of the biomass. Pasture land is only 40 per cent as productive as this average whereas forest land is 20 per cent above average productivity. Forest land for carbon sequestration is considered to have the same productivity.

Due to historic settlement patterns, the authors consider the use of built land as equivalent to a reduction in arable land area.

Accounting for sea space productivity is slightly more complex. Seafood yields per hectare of ocean are low compared to land-based biomass production. One reason is that fish are higher up the food chain than land-based sources of protein. Originally, the authors accounted for sea space by direct reference to its true physical area. This led to some criticisms that the footprint was being unduly inflated. More recently we have preferred to account for seafood consumption in terms of the equivalent (and much smaller) area of land required to produce the same amount (in calorific terms) of white meat. We fondly refer to these as 'sea chickens'.

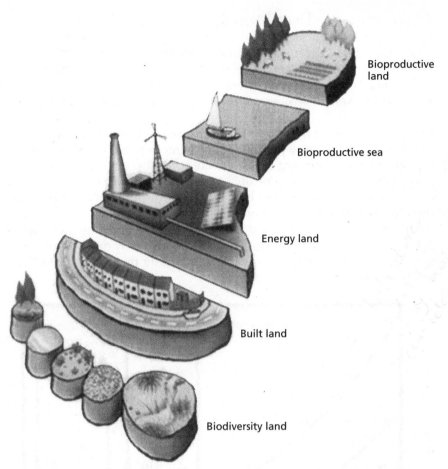

Figure 4.2 *Broad land categories used in ecological footprint analysis*

energy demands. Depending on energy policy, the area and type of this land will vary. For example, we can offset the release of CO_2 from fossil-fuel burning by setting aside land (in perpetuity) for growing trees which reabsorb, or sequester, the carbon emissions. However, at the present time an insignificant forest area is set aside to absorb the pollution arising from our use of fossil fuel.[5] There are signs that this will slowly change with the implementation of the Kyoto Protocol.[6] As has been noted earlier (see Box 3.2), sequestering CO_2 in this manner is – at best – a short-term solution. Later the authors present ecological footprint data for a range of fossil and non-fossil fuel energy sources.

- Biodiversity land. This is defined as the land needed to ensure the protection of the planet's 15 million, or so, non-human species. This is dealt with in the next section.

FAIR SHARES FOR ALL?

*'Ten billion [people] with everyone following an American diet ...
would require 9 billion tonnes of grain, the harvest of more than
four planets at Earth's current output levels... achieving even
modest gains is becoming difficult'* (State of the World 1999)[7]

Few would disagree that there are currently massive inequities in the
global economy. Twenty per cent of the planet's population is currently
responsible for 86 per cent of the private consumption expenditure; the
poorest 20 per cent are responsible for a minute 1.3 per cent.[8]

Given that the amount of land available for humanity is finite, and
thus the available productivity ultimately bounded, issues of resource
equity cannot easily be ignored. As the authors demonstrate in Chapter
7, bioproductive capacity is unevenly appropriated by different nations,
with the richer countries generally demanding more per capita than
the poorer ones.

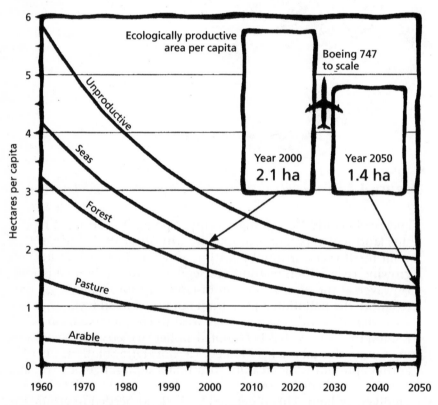

Note: Assumes current land and sea productivity is maintained (an optimistic prediction)

Figure 4.3 *Land and sea availability per capita projected to 2050 based on
medium variant population projections*

If nature's capital is truly our global commons then some level of redistribution is required. To express this concept, Wackernagel and Rees introduced the notion of the earthshare – the average amount of ecologically productive land and sea available globally per capita. Table 4.1 summarizes the amount of each land type available globally and shows the earthshare for each land type based on Year 2000 population data. Further to this, Figure 4.3 projects land availability per capita to the year 2050 based on a population projection of 9.5 billion (non-productive land such as ice-covered and desert lands are included as 'Unproductive').

The calculations in Table 4.1 show that an average earthshare for land plus sea is around 2.1 ha. Of course, this is a very anthropocentric view and land needs to be set aside for the 15 million, or so, other species that share this planet. How much land our flora and fauna require is a moot point but, as we have seen, the current rate of extinctions provides a powerful argument for increasing the amount of protected land over and above current levels.

According to the World Commission on Environment and Development, at least 12 per cent of the ecological capacity, representing all ecosystem types, should be preserved for biodiversity protection.[9] This 12 per cent may not be enough for securing biodiver-

---

Box 4.2 Is 12 Per Cent Enough for Securing Biodiversity?

Many ecologists believe that much more than 12 per cent of the world's ecosystems needs to be preserved in order to secure biodiversity.[10] For example, in 1970 ecologist Eugene Odum recommended, in the case of the State of Georgia, that 40 per cent of the territory remain as natural area, while 10 per cent be ceded to urban-industrial systems, 30 per cent to food growing and 20 per cent to fibre production. Wildlife ecologist and scientific director of the Wildlands Project, Reed Noss (1991a, 1991b) hypothesized that about 50 per cent of an average region needs to be protected as wilderness (or equivalent core reserves and lightly used buffer zones) to restore populations of large carnivores and meet other conservation goals.

Reed Noss and Allen Cooperrider (1994), after reviewing several studies, concluded that most regions will need protection of some 25 to 75 per cent of their total land area in core reserves and inner buffer zones, assuming that this space is distributed optimally with regard to representation of biodiversity and viability of species, and well connected within the region and to other reserve networks in neighbouring regions.

To put the matter in perspective, around 3.5 per cent of global land area is currently 'totally' protected.[11] The actual figure may be somewhat less than this, as the 'protected' areas often include parks and wildlife reserves where considerable human activity still prevails or pollution impacts on the ecosystems.

Table 4.1 *Average Per Capita Earthshare based on Populations of 6 and 9.5 billion*

Land type	Global area (billion ha)	Average earthshare (ha/per cap)	
		Population 6 billion	Population 9.5 billion
Arable	1.45	0.24	0.15
Pasture	3.36	0.56	0.35
Forest	5.12	0.85	0.54
Productive Sea	2.90	0.48	0.31
Total land and sea		2.13	1.35
Total minus biodiversity area (at 12 per cent)		1.87	1.19
(at 25 per cent)		1.60	1.01

sity, but conserving more will require political courage and commitment over and above that currently in evidence.

Accepting 12 per cent as the magic target for biodiversity preservation, it becomes apparent that humanity must learn to live equitably within a footprint of around 2 ha (about 4.5 acres). Assuming a population increase to 9.5 billion, this figure will drop to just under 1.2 ha (roughly three acres).

If we acknowledge that perhaps Noss and Cooperrider's lower figure of 25 per cent of set aside for biodiversity is more realistic, then the land available for human uses reduces to 1.6 ha now and a little over 1 ha with a population of 9.5 billion (4.0 and 2.5 acres respectively).

The reality of living in a finite world is stark. Imagine a square field representing the current average earthshare. Close to one half of the field would be forested, just under one-quarter would be pasture and just over one-tenth arable land. The remainder would be covered in water excepting a small area, similar in size to the arable portion, which is given over to other species. Standing in the centre of this field you would clearly be able to view the boundary less than 75 m away. A leisurely walk around the perimeter of the field (600 m) would take you about ten minutes.

If you, or your child, went back to the field in 2050, it would be noticeably more cramped. The edge would now be 15 m closer to your vantage point and a stroll around the perimeter would take less than eight minutes.

We live in a shrinking world. The inescapable conclusion is that we must learn to live a quality life with less.

COMPOUND AND COMPONENT-BASED APPROACHES TO CALCULATION

There are two complementary approaches to calculating ecological footprints. The authors have termed these the compound and component-based methods. These are briefly described below.

Compound Calculation

The compound approach to the calculation of footprints, devised by Mathis Wackernagel, is the more inclusive and robust method. Taking its primary unit of analysis as the nation state, consumption is calculated by reference to trade flows and energy data.

The calculation is composed of three main parts. The first part consists of a consumption analysis of over 50 biotic resources including meat, dairy produce, fruit, vegetables, pulses, grains, tobacco, coffee, wood products, and so on. Consumption is calculated by adding imports to production and subtracting exports. Where necessary, further adjustments are made to avoid double counting across categories. For example, grain-fed animals are accounted for by feed consumption (as arable land) rather than by grazed pasture land. Using FAO estimates of world average yield, consumption is translated into appropriated ecologically productive area. In other words, the consumption quantities are divided by their corresponding (world average) biotic productivity which gives the arable, pasture, or forest land and productive sea areas necessary to sustain this consumption.

The second part of the calculation determines the energy balance – considering both locally generated energy and that embodied in over 100 categories of traded goods. Where the primary fuel used is known, this is adjusted for carbon content. This portion of the calculation is used to derive the energy footprint – usually the amount of forested land necessary to sequester the CO_2 emissions.

The final part of the calculation summarizes the ecological footprint in six ecological categories and gives the total, presented as per capita figures. Multiplying the per capita data by the country's population gives the total footprint of the nation. An adjustment is also made to express the result in world average productive land. 'Equivalence factors' are used to scale the land categories in proportion to their productivities (see Box 4.2). The total is then compared with an estimate of how much biocapacity exists within the country. The actual land area is adjusted by a 'yield factor' to equate local productivity of each land category to the global average. This scales the national areas in proportion to their true productivities. The total area of bioproductive land is reduced by 12 per cent to account for biodiversity needs. The remaining 88 per cent is referred to as the 'available area'.

As an example, some consumption data for Costa Rica (population 3,424,000) is presented. Tables 4.2, 4.3 and 4.4 show a simplified version of the calculations for this country. Table 4.2 shows the accounting for the biotic resources, Table 4.3 the primary and embodied energy calculations and Table 4.4 the summary results.

COMPONENT-BASED CALCULATION

In the component-based model the ecological footprint values for certain activities are pre-calculated using data appropriate to the region under consideration. For example, to calculate the impact of car travel data on fuel consumption, manufacturing and maintenance energy, land take and distance travelled are sourced for the region in question – then an average ecological footprint estimate is derived for a single passenger-km or other appropriate unit (see Table 4.5). This can then be used to calculate the impact of vehicle use at the individual, organizational or regional level as required. The land categories originally proposed by Wackernagel and Rees (1996) are essentially retained – energy land, built (or degraded) land, bioproductive land, sea and biodiversity land.

The same calculation process as shown for car travel can equally well be undertaken for other forms of travel as well as primary energy usage, waste production, food consumption and so on. What basic life cycle data that can be found is collated and converted to derive the footprint for that component.

The aim is to account for most consumption with a series of component analyses. For example, when calculating the ecological footprint of an organization or region, the authors typically look at the 24 components set out in Table 4.6.

The authors' experience of comparing the sum total of these components with the compound footprinting results is that they capture the vast majority of anthropogenic impacts. Furthermore, according to the sensitivity required, components such as food might be subdivided further or categories omitted when they are not applicable. To avoid double counting the energy used for the production and transportation of goods for example, the values for primary energy use and freight transport are adjusted based on assumptions about the sources of embodied energy. Similarly, adjustments are made to eliminate the double counting of built land.

Of course, data sources rarely agree. For example, the average amount of CO_2 produced by a tonne-km transported by air is variously given as 795 g,[12] 1206 g[13] and 1642 g.[14] Estimates are based on different assumptions, methodologies and samples. Part of the component-based methodology therefore involves a sensitivity analysis using different data sources to determine the most representative figures. To give an example, Table 4.7 shows the variation in data sources for the embodied energy and built land associated with wind-generated power. Table 4.8 shows a range of possible ecological footprint results depending on which combination of sources is used.

When compared with the compound approach to ecological footprinting, the component approach has certain advantages and disadvantages. In its favour, it is easier to communicate and is more instructive. The breakdown of impacts by activity has a definite appeal to those involved in policy-making or education. The disadvantages can mainly be traced to problems with data variability and reliability, which make national and international comparisons problematic. Calculating the direct and indirect life cycle impacts is highly data-intensive – quite small changes in assumptions and data sources can lead to differing results. The need to carefully consider the life cycle effects of each component in detail is a definite barrier to widespread adoption of this method.

WORK IN PROGRESS

The authors acknowledge that neither compound nor component-based calculation methods tell the whole story. Both omit some uses of nature for resource production and waste absorption, and they both suffer from data availability and accuracy problems to varying degrees. The ease with which they can identify trends and monitor changes also differs between the two methods.

One important resource that is not included in most current footprint assessments is fresh water. The authors discuss methods for the measurement of water catchment areas in Chapter 5. The ecological impacts of contamination are also only partly included in current assessments. Contamination, manifested in industrial areas of the former Soviet Union for example, or in the many areas adversely affected by acid rain all over the world, can significantly reduce ecological productivity or make products of nature unfit for human use. By not including them, current results are underestimates of human use of nature. In Chapter 10 the authors discuss two tentative approaches to the inclusion of a range of other pollutants into the footprinting methodology.[15]

Data, ideally on a life cycle basis, are necessary for the component-based approach, and these data are often simply not available. This is also a problem – to a lesser extent – with the compound calculation method. Most traded, manufactured goods are currently only accounted for in terms of their embodied energy – other resource use and waste discharges are currently not included. The accuracy of the footprint calculation is often diminished by the necessary use of proxy data and assumptions about activities or resource use. For example,

Table 4.2 *Annual Consumption of Biotic Resources: Costa Rica (1995)*

Resource	Global yield	Production	Import
Unit	(kg per ha)	(t)	(t)
MEAT		180,000	967
Fresh meat			875
Beef, buffalo meat	32	92,232	400
Sheep, goat meat	72	22	3
Non-bovine, non- goat, non-mutton, non-buffalo	764	87,746	564
DAIRY PRODUCE			
Milk	458	539,000	0
Cheese	46	6000	250
Butter	22	4000	0
Eggs	573		0
MARINE FISH	35		
CEREALS	2752	206,000	588,400
Wheat and flour			164,800
Rice			72,730
Maize			350,000
FRUIT & VEGETABLES	8136	3,297,000	12,396
Fresh tomatoes			0
Onions			0
Hops			1
Oranges, tangerines, clementines			0
Lemons and limes			0
Other citrus			0
Bananas			0
Apples			6945
Grapes			2975
Raisins			330
Pears			707
Peaches			1438
Fresh pineapples			0
Dates			0
ANIMAL FEED	2752		0
ROOTS & TUBERS	12,814	209,000	1600
PULSES	802	28,000	16,000

Note: Not all categories of biotic resources are listed in this sample table. Download
the full spreadsheet from www.ecologicalfootprint.com

Export	Apparent consumption	Net imported, manufactured products	Footprint component	Land category
(t)	(t)	(t)	(ha/per cap)	
24,860				
23,790				
21,410	71,222		0.6529	Pasture
180	−155		−0.0006	Pasture
3270		−2706	−0.0010	Arable
12,968	526,032		0.3355	Pasture
189		61	0.0004	Pasture
81		−81	−0.0011	Pasture
0		0	0.0000	Arable
	6		0.1846	Sea
7000	787,400		0.0836	Arable
600				
4640				
1700				
2,461,512	847,884		0.0304	Arable
104				
5069				
0				
331				
130				
14				
2,284,825				
31				
25				
5				
6				
2				
170,958				
12				
0		0	0.0000	Arable
330	210,270		0.0048	Arable
3675	40,325		0.0147	Arable

Table 4.3 *Annual Consumption of Primary Energy and the Net Embodied Energy in Imports: Costa Rica (1995)*

Primary energy use	Global average energy to land ratio	Energy use	Footprint component	Land type
Unit	(Gj/ha/yr)	(Gj per cap)	(ha per cap)	
Coal consumption:	55	0.00	0.0000	Energy land
Liquid fossil fuel consumption:	71	24.23	0.3413	Energy land
Fossil gas consumption:	93	0.00	0.0000	Energy land
Total fossil fuel consumption:		24.23		
Nuclear energy consumption (thermal):	71	0.00	0.0000	Energy land
Energy embodied in net imported goods:	71	15.94	0.2245	Energy land
Hydro-electricity consumption:	1000	3.81	0.0038	Built-up area

Embodied energy calculations	Energy intensity (Gj/tonne)	Import (tonnes)	Export (tonnes)	Embodied energy (Pj)
BEVERAGES & TOBACCO	10	10,079	0	0.10
Alcoholic beverages	15	6496	0	
Tobacco and manufactures	100	0	0	
Crude tobacco	10	453	272	
CRUDE MATERIALS		0	0	
Hides, skins	10	0	196	0.00
Rubber, crude	20	12,142	0	0.24
Wood, shaped	10	0	0	0.00
Pulp & waste paper	15	0	0	0.00
TEXTILE FIBRES	15	0	0	0.00
MINERALS	1	0	0	0.00
METAL ORES	2	0	0	0.00
METAL SCRAP	50			0.00
Iron and steel ores	50	0	0	0.00
CRUDE ANIMAL & VEGETABLE	10	0	70,594	−0.71

Note: Not all embodied energy categories are listed in this sample table. Download the full spreadsheet from www.ecologicalfootprint.com

Great tables. Very understandable more understandable for the biologist.

Footprinting Fundamentals 73

Table 4.4 *Summary Results of Per Capita Demand and Capacity: Costa Rica (1995)*

Demand – Footprint (per capita)

Category Unit	Total (ha per cap)	Equivalence factor	Equivalent total (ha per cap)
Fossil energy	0.57	1.17	0.66
Built-up area	0.02	2.83	0.05
Arable land	0.35	2.83	0.99
Pasture	1.10	0.44	0.48
Forest including deforestation	0.51	1.17	0.60
Sea	0.18	0.06	0.01
Total used	2.73		2.80

Supply – Existing national biocapacity (per capita)

Category	Yield factor	National area (ha per cap)	Yield adjusted equivalent area (ha per cap)
CO_2 absorption land		0.00	0.00
Built-up area	1.22	0.01	0.05
Arable land	1.22	0.15	0.54
Pasture	1.63	0.74	0.53
Forest	2.11	0.40	0.98
Sea	1.00	2.48	0.16
Total existing		3.80	2.25
Total available	(minus 12 per cent for biodiversity)		1.98

accuracy could also be improved by analysing fossil energy in finer categories. The CO_2 release per energy unit, for example, can vary by a factor of two.

Even where data are available, their accuracy is often suspect. Not all national statistics are equally reliable. In the UN, for example, there are discrepancies between the same data reported in different publications. As data availability and accuracy improve, so will the accuracy of the footprint.

The key merit of the compound method is its easy replicability. By using the same assumptions for all assessments, the results for different countries are comparable in relative terms. It is also sufficiently detailed to give a general indication of the magnitude of human impact globally. Since the compound method captures the resources that are used up in a country – independent of the activity they are used for – it is most effective at capturing indirect effects. But this advantage can also be a

LIVERPOOL JOHN MOORES UNIVERSITY
LEARNING SERVICES

Table 4.5 *Ecological Footprint Estimate for UK Car Travel (ha Per Annual Passenger km)*[16]

| Component data | Demand (per 10,000 passenger km/yr) | | | | |
	ha		Land type	Equivalence factor	Equivalent total ha
Petrol consumption	0.094 litres/km 0.22 kg CO_2/km	0.42[a]	fossil energy	1.17	0.49[a]
Maintenance & manufacture	0.042 litres/km 0.10 kg CO_2/km equivalent	0.19[b]	fossil energy	1.17	0.22[b]
Road space	2,581,747 ha	0.06[c]	built-up area	2.83	0.17[c]
Car road share	86%				
UK annual car travel	362,400,000,000 km				
Car occupancy	1.6 persons[d]				
Footprint calculation	(a+b+c)/d	**0.42**			**0.56**

disadvantage in that the activities that cause particular resource consumption and waste production cannot easily be distinguished.

In contrast, the component-based approach has a more pedagogical, or instructive, structure. This increases the face validity of footprinting at the local and personal level. The activity-based model has the added advantage of facilitating data collection where detailed resource usage statistics are not available. The main disadvantage of the component-based approach is that it relies heavily on information about the resource intensities of the included activities (as noted earlier). This makes it less sensitive to changes in technology but more suitable to the monitoring and management of behavioural changes.

The analysis method you choose depends on the accuracy you require and the features of the item being measured. In Chapter 5 the authors present the main conversion factors necessary to undertake a component-based ecological footprint analysis. Chapter 7 describes the compound footprint analysis as applied to the Footprint of Nations study. A good example of the component-based approach is the calculation of Oxfordshire's footprint in Chapter 8. Spreadsheets that illustrate both compound and component-based analyses are available on the internet.[18]

Calculators at the ready – the time has come to get your feet wet!

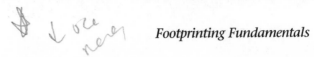

Table 4.6 *List of Component Impacts Usually Considered on an Annual Basis when Undertaking a Component-based Ecological Footprint Analysis of a Region or Organization*

Components	
Electricity (GWh) – domestic	Food (t)
Gas (GWh) – domestic	Wood products (m³)
Electricity – other (GWh)	Travel by car (Passenger '000 km)
Gas – other (GWh)	Travel by bus (Passenger '000 km)
Recycled waste glass (t)	Travel by train (Passenger '000 km)
Recycled waste paper and card (t)	Travel by air (Passenger '000 km)
Recycled waste metals (t)	Road haulage ('000 t-km)
Recycled waste compost (t)	Rail freight ('000 t-km)
Recycled – other domestic waste (t)	Sea freight ('000 t-km)
Waste – household (t)	Air freight ('000 t-km)
Waste – commercial (paper, metal etc) (t)	Water – household (m³)
Waste – inert (brick, concrete etc) (t)	

Note: Indicated in brackets are the most common units of measurement. Consideration is also given to the land taken out of bioproductive use

Table 4.7 *Differing Values for the Embodied Energy and Built Land Associated with Wind Power*[17]

Component	Data Embodied energy (Mwh/GWh)	References
Embodied energy	142	Stelzer (1994)
Range of values is	44	
attributable to	36	
different construction	27	Derived from American
methods, wind	11	Wind Energy Association
generator ratings,		(AWEA) (1998)
and sitings		

	Built-upon land (ha/GWh/yr)	
Built-upon land		
Range of values is	0.6	Derived from AWEA (1998)
attributable to	0.29	Wackernagel & Rees (1996)
different figures on	0.15	Stelzer (1994)
the land take (tower	0.11	Worldwatch Institute
foundations, servicing		(1995)
roads etc) associated		
with a wind generator		

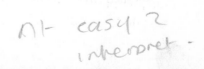

Table 4.8 *Ecological Footprint Results Obtained from Differing Data Sources Assuming that Fossil Fuel-based Electricity is Used for Wind Generator Construction (see note 17)*

Footprint (ha/GWh/yr)	Reference Data
3	AWEA low embodied energy estimate with Wackernagel & Rees land use estimate
8	AWEA high embodied energy estimate with AWEA derived land use estimate
27	Stelzer high estimate for energy with Stelzer land use
5	AWEA middle estimate for energy with Worldwatch land use estimate
9	Stelzer low estimate for energy with Stelzer land use

QUESTIONS

- Does the footprint provide a precise estimate of human impact? (see Chapter 6, Question 5)
- If not, don't we need a more accurate policy tool? (see Chapter 6, Question 6)
- The ecological footprint does not appear to recognize that as technology improves we can cope with more people and less land per capita. For example, we have adapted our agricultural systems to produce more food per hectare and scientists have responded to the reductions in sea fish stocks by farming fish in ponds and estuaries. Why can't this continue? (see Chapter 6, Question 17)
- What can ecological footprint analysis tell us about the future of the planet – are we all doomed? (see Chapter 6, Question 20)

NOTES

1   Cited in 'Revisiting Carrying Capacity: Area-based Indicators of Sustainability', by William E Rees, 1996, *Population and Environment*, vol 17, no 3, originally from 'Carrying Capacity and the limits to freedom', paper prepared for the Social Ecology Session 1, 11th World Congress of Sociology, New Delhi, India

2   From Inge Røpke's contribution to 'Monetary Analysis: turning a blind eye on sustainability', Rees and Wackernagel, 1999, *Ecological Economics*, vol 29, no 1

3   *State of the World 1998*, p63, Earthscan

4   Wackernagel, M and Yount, J D, 1998, 'The Ecological Footprint: An Indicator of Progress Toward Regional Sustainability', p4, *Environmental Monitoring and Assessment*, vol 51, pp511–529

5   The UK Department of the Environment, Transport, and the Regions has published environmental reporting guidelines for business based around

greenhouse gas emissions (DETR, 1999, *Environmental reporting: guidelines for company reporting on greenhouse gas emissions*). These are based on the measurement of the carbon dioxide equivalence of the six main types of greenhouse gases as covered in the Kyoto Protocol. An online carbon emissions calculator for the key energy sources is maintained by Best Foot Forward (http://www.bestfootforward.com)

6   Mattoon, A T, 'Bogging down in the sinks', 1998, Worldwatch

7   *State of the World 1999*, p15. The United Nations projection shows that 10 billion people is a possibility as early as 2040 (high prediction)

8   *Human Development Report 1998*, UN Development Programme, OUP, p3

9   The World Commission on Environment and Development, *Our Common Future*, Oxford, Oxford University Press, 1987, p147, p166

10 For more detailed discussion see Reed F Noss, 1991, 'From endangered species to biodiversity', pp227–246, in K A Kohm, (ed), 1991, *Balancing on the Brink of Extinction: The Endangered Species Act and Lessons for the Future*, Washington, DC: Island Press; Reed F Noss, 1991, 'Sustainability and wilderness', *Conservation Biology*, pp120–121; Reed F Noss and Allen Y Cooperrider, 1994, *Saving Nature's Legacy – Protecting and Restoring Biodiversity*, Washington DC: Island Press; Eugene P Odum, 1970, 'Optimum population and environment: A Georgia microcosm', *Current History*, 58, pp355–359

11 *World Resources 98–99*, p320. Figure given is for IUCN categories I–III.

12 'Annual Environmental Report', British Airways, 1996

13 *Critical Mass: Transport, Environment and Society in the Twenty-first Century* Whitelegg, J, 1997, Pluto Press, London

14 Derived from Whitelegg, 1997, op cit and 'Greenhouse Gas Inventory Revised guidelines for National Greenhouse Gas Inventories', Intergovernmental Panel on Climate Change, 1996, IPCC Secretariat, c/o World Meteorological Organisation, Geneva, Switzerland

15 Other writers have looked at the footprinting of pollution. See, for example, Folke, C, Jansson, Å, Larsson, J, Costanza, R, 'Ecosystem Appropriation by Cities', *Ambio* 26(3), May 1997; Kautsky, N, Berg, H, Folke, C, and Troell, M, 'Ecological Footprint of Shrimp and Tilapia Aquaculture' in *The Fourth Asian Fisheries Forum*, Eds Zhou, Y, Zhou, H, Yao, C, Lu, Y, Hu, F, Ciu, H, Din, F Beijing, 1997, pp754 and 'Ecological footprint for assessment of resource use and development limitations in shrimp and tilapia aquaculture', Kautsky, N, Berg, H, Folke, C, Larsson, J, and Troell, M, *Aquaculture Research* 1997 28, pp753–766. See also the work on the Sustainable Process Index (Chapter 10)

16 Sources: 'Transport Statistics Great Britain' Department of the Environment, Transport and the Regions (DETR), 1997, London, The Stationery Office; 'Road Facts 98' British Road Federation, 1998, BRF; BFF personal communication with DETR regarding National Travel Survey, 1999; *Our Ecological Footprint*, Wackernagel and Rees, 1996, New Society. Note conversion to footprint uses a CO_2 sequestration rate of 0.52kg per m^2

17 American Wind Energy Association, 1998, downloaded on 30 March 1999 from *Wind Energy Weekly* at http://www.awea.org/faq/bal.html; Stelzer, T and Wiese, A, 1994, Ganzheitliche Bilanzierung der Stromerzeugung aus erneuerbaren Energieträgern, 9 in Friends of the Earth Europe, 1995, *Towards Sustainable Europe: The Study*, Friends of the

Earth Netherlands, Amsterdam; Wackernagel, M and Rees, W, 1996, *Our Ecological Footprint: reducing human impact upon the earth*, New Society Publishers, Gabriola Island, BC, Canada; *State of the World 1995*, Brown, L (ed) Worldwatch Institute, W W Norton, New York

18   See the web sites of Redefining Progress: http://www.rprogress.org; and Best Foot Forward: http://www.bestfootforward.com

Chapter 5

From Activities to Impacts

- what impact have we made on the earth

This chapter shows how to calculate simple ecological footprints for a range of different activities, such as energy and materials use, travelling, eating and waste generation.

These are presented in such a way as to make ecological footprint analysis more accessible to community and Local Agenda 21 groups, local authorities, corporations and organizations, individuals and others without access to detailed resource and pollution data.

In each section are one or more data tables containing footprint conversion factors. To reduce the range of possible values, the authors have made some simplifying assumptions (see Box 5.1) which are summarized in the appropriate table. Each section also has one, or more, worked examples to illustrate the thinking behind the calculation of the ecological footprint conversion factors.

To allow for meaningful comparisons, the conversion factors all refer to the productive area that would need to be appropriated per annum – that is, the number of hectares required to produce in one year what was consumed in that year.

ENERGY

'If sunbeams were weapons of war we would have had solar power long ago' (George Porter, British chemist)

One resource that lubricates our industrial economy more than any other is energy. Fossil fuels – coal, oil and gas – are the primary sources of this power. These fuels together account for around 90 per cent of the commercial energy used in industrialized countries and about 75 per cent of usage worldwide (see Table 5.1).

The days of a fossil fuel-dependent economy are, however, numbered. A switch to renewable sources of energy is essential if we are to avoid unacceptable climate change, undesirable effects on health,

---

Box 5.1 Health Warning: Global Generalizations

Global average data have been used or reasonably estimated throughout, except where indicated. The calculations presented in this chapter thus provide a good indication of environmental impact which is comparable between different countries and regions.

The results are expressed in hectare years of world average productive space to facilitate comparisons and to show what share of global ecological productivity each activity appropriates.

Where a range of values is given, this is usually due to data differences. For example, concrete may be produced in different countries with varying energy efficiencies. Similarly, transportation impacts are likely to be more significant in the larger countries or in those that rely heavily on imports. Average vehicle occupancy rates might change from region to region, as will fuel efficiencies and road use statistics. In most cases a reasonable working estimate can be obtained by taking the mid-point of the range given.

For a more accurate footprint result the authors recommend an in-depth analysis to determine actual energy and materials use.

---

and thoughtfully manage the depletion of our fossil fuel reserves. The jury is out as to which of these factors will play the leading role, but all are currently the subject of much investigation and speculation.

Some estimates suggest that oil reserves may already be half gone – with a peak production predicted in about 2010. Even if we had ample remaining reserves of oil, as well as gas and coal, it may be wise not to release all of it as carbon into the atmosphere.[1]

Various strategies have been proposed to wean the world off fossil fuels and offset the most negative aspects of their usage. Taking centre stage are the renewable energy sources: solar, wind, hydro and wave, biomass, and the so-called fifth fuel, energy conservation.

Afforestation has also received much attention as a means to sequestrate, or reabsorb, the carbon emissions from fossil-fuel combus-

Table 5.1 *Global Energy Use by Source (1997)*

Energy source	Total (million tonnes of oil equivalent)[2]	Share (per cent)
Coal	2133	22
Oil	2940	30
Natural gas	2173	23
Nuclear	579	6
Renewables*	1833	19
Total	9647	100

Note: * Includes biomass, wind, hydro, geothermal and solar energy

---

Box 5.2 Derivation Example – 'Footprints in the Wind'

Let us consider the footprint for a wind generator.

Several different estimates exist for the energy required to build and maintain a wind generator. These are, of course, partly dependent on the size and location of the generator. The American Wind Energy Association (AWEA) provides estimates for three different installations (11MWh, 27MWh and 36MWh) of the energy required to produce and maintain a wind generator per GWh of energy produced.[3] These are slightly lower than other published figures, which range from 44MWh to 142MWh per GWh.[4] This is possibly because the former reflect more up to date construction methods and materials. Based on our review of the literature, the middle AWEA estimate is thought to be the most generally applicable.

Assuming that this energy was supplied using EU standard electricity, we get a footprint by multiplying the embodied energy required by the footprint for EU electricity.

Energy land: 27/1000*161 = 4.3 ha per GWh of delivered electricity per year, where:

> 27 is the number of MWh of embodied energy per GWh of energy produced
> 1000 is the conversion from MWh to GWh
> 161 is the global average land ha/yr figure per GWh of EU (hard coal) grid electricity (from Table 5.2 – which includes equivalence factor)

A number of estimates of the direct land required by a wind generator (the space taken up by the generator foundations and access roads, for example) have also been published. These fall within the range of 0.1–0.6 ha per GWh of delivered electricity. Most are close to the lower figure with, for example, estimates by Wackernagel[5] at 0.3 ha/GWh and Stelzer[6] at 0.2 ha/GWh. However, to be cautious we use the higher figure from AWEA.[7] For comparative purposes this can then be turned into global average productive space.

Built land: = 0.6 * 2.8 = 1.7 ha per GWh of delivered electricity per year, where:

> 0.6 is the degraded land estimate; and
> 2.8 is the equivalence factor for built-up land

Adding the energy-land footprint to the built-land footprint gives a total wind energy footprint of:

> 4.3 + 1.7 = 6.0 ha per GWh per year.

---

tion. This is, however, a 'one shot' solution as only new-growth forests are net CO_2 absorbers and the amount of land that could reasonably be planted out would offset, it is estimated, only one-and-a-half years

Table 5.2 *Delivered Energy Footprint Factors for a Number of Renewable and Non-renewable Sources*

Energy: primary and secondary fuels	Footprint (hectare years per GWh)	Assumptions
Natural gas (mains)	45	Based on IPCC 1996 data
Fuel oil	59	Assumes direct use of oil. Based on IPCC 1996 data
Fuel wood	93 to 97	Using global dry wood yields. Converted from tonnes to GWh using IPCC net calorific value for oven-dried wood
Bottled gas (LPG)	51	Based on IPCC 1996 data

worth of anthropogenic emissions.[8] Nonetheless, it seems likely that the negotiations arising out of the Kyoto Protocol and subsequent deliberations at the Buenos Aires Climate Summit in 1998 will continue to focus policy-makers on this relatively painless and inexpensive alternative to wholesale fossil fuel reductions.[9]

It is possible to calculate an ecological footprint value for a range of fossil and renewable fuels (see Box 5.2 for a derivation example). This is based on their direct land use and the land required to sequestrate any carbon emitted, either directly from combustion or indirectly to construct or maintain the generating device (for example solar panel or wind generator)

The footprint conversion factors for a range of energy sources are shown in Tables 5.2 and 5.3. These are already adjusted to provide a result in global average productive space (expressed in hectare years). To compare, for example, the footprint of 1 MWh (1/1000th of a GWh) of grid electricity (generated by fossil fuels) with the same amount generated by renewable solar energy, multiply the footprint conversion factor by the energy figure:

Grid electricity = 161/1000 = 0.161 ha per MWh per year
Solar = 24/1000 = 0.024 ha per MWh per year

TRAVEL

'A journey of a thousand miles begins with a single step'
(Chinese Proverb)

The world is shrinking as new and faster forms of travel are devised. The size of the world is now perceived as being 20 times smaller than it did to a traveller of 100 years ago.[10]

Table 5.3 *Delivered Electricity Footprint Factors for a Number of Renewable and Non-renewable Sources*[11]

Energy: electricity generation	Footprint (hectare years per GWh)	Assumptions
Electricity produced using hard coal condensing power stations	161	This is the predominant source of electricity within the EU although countries vary significantly. The figure is similar to the US fuel mix for grid electricity
Electricity produced using coal	198	Based on UK data. This estimate will vary depending on the coal source and generation technology. See hard coal figure above
Electricity produced using oil	150	Based on UK data
Electricity produced using natural gas	94	Based on UK data
Wind	6	A reasonable estimate taking into account embodied energy for construction and direct land use. A high estimate can bring the footprint up to 27 hectares per year GWh. It is assumed that the energy used to construct the wind turbine is fossil fuel-derived electricity. Using wind energy for manufacture would significantly reduce the footprint
Photovoltaics	24	This estimate accounts for manufacturing energy and land use. The embodied energy data quoted for photovoltaic cells range widely. The estimate presented here is based upon cadmium telluride (CdTe) & copper indium selenide (CIS) cells. Again, it is assumed that fossil fuel-derived electricity is used for construction. Using solar energy for manufacture would significantly reduce the footprint
Biomass – woody	27 to 46	This estimate is calculated from the forest land necessary to grow the required fuel. It varies from the fuelwood estimate due to the increased yields through managed biomass plantations
Hydroelectricity	10 to 75	Footprint can vary significantly depending on the type of installation. The top-end figure of 75 is based on a Californian mix of 96 per cent low altitude and 4 per cent high altitude installations. It is assumed that the embodied energy is fossil fuel-derived electricity

---

Box 5.3 Get Your Cheap Flights Here

Have you tried searching the web for bargain airfares? Your search is over – point your browser to www.chooseclimate.org. Just two clicks on the map on this web site will show you the real cost of any flight.

If you are looking to travel to a warmer climate, then flying is one of the fastest and cheapest ways to cook the planet. CO_2, NO_x, and H_2O emissions from aircraft contribute substantially to the greenhouse effect.

Source: Adapted from Ben Matthews' home page: last accessed 25 November 1999

Consider, as an example, crossing the Atlantic. In 1854 the American clipper, *James Baines*, set a longstanding record by crossing in 12 days 6 hours from Boston to Liverpool using solely the power of the wind. Today, Concorde routinely flies business passengers from London to New York in less than four hours, making a day trip to the US a practical possibility. Such rapid transit is not without its natural-resource implications, for all of the 100 passengers will effectively use 20 times their own body weight in aviation fuel to make the return trip.[12]

This increase in mobility has clearly led to increases in the distances people are willing, able and expected to travel. Even in a relatively small and compact country such as the UK, the average daily distance travelled by car has increased from 14 km in 1975 to 22 km in 1996.[13]

Therefore it is perhaps not surprising that the transport sector is the fastest growing source of CO_2 emissions worldwide.[14] Road-building has also led to a significant land take, both directly and as part of the process of urbanization. For example, each 100 km of motorway requires about 260 ha of land.[15]

There are, of course, also a myriad of health and social problems that have been attributed to the increase in mobility – road accidents, the fragmentation of communities, road rage, the rise in respiratory problems and the loss of tranquillity, for example.

In calculating the ecological footprint for travel there are many factors to consider. They include mode of travel, fuel efficiency (for construction, maintenance and use), vehicle occupancy rates and travel conditions (weather, congestion) for example. Based on data from a variety of sources as indicated, the authors have derived the footprint figures set out in Tables 5.5 and 5.6 for passenger and freight transport respectively. Included is land for carbon sequestration and for building uses such as roads, railway lines and airports.

Box 5.4 Derivation Example – 'Tyre Treads'

Let us consider the ecological footprint for car travel.

The majority of the footprint is concerned with the energy used in manufacturing, maintaining and fuelling the car. These figures are then translated into CO_2 emissions and converted to the associated land area needed to sequester the carbon. One estimate of manufacturing and maintenance energy is that given by Wackernagel and Rees.[16] They estimated that the equivalent of 15 per cent of the fuel energy use is needed to manufacture and maintain a vehicle with an extra 30 per cent for the construction and maintenance of the road infrastructure. The authors refer to this as the 'uplift factor'.

Turning to fuel consumption, in the UK 99 per cent of cars are petrol and 1 per cent are diesel.[17] Here we use the petrol consumption of the average car, which is reported as 11km/litre.[18] Therefore, one estimate of the energy footprint per car-kilometre is:

Energy land: (1/11) * 1.45 * 2.36 * 1.92 = 0.62

0.62 * 1.17 = 0.73 m^2 per car-kilometre per year, where:

1/11 converts kilometres per litre to litres per kilometre of petrol.
1.45 is the uplift factor.
2.36 is the weight of CO_2 in kilogrammes produced per litre of petrol.
1.92 is the area (m^2) of average forest land required to sequester one kilogramme of CO_2 per year.
1.17 is the equivalence factor for forest land.

In addition, the car requires built-up land. For this we need three data points. First, there is the length of the road network, which is widely reported by governments. Secondly, there is road width – this is more difficult to ascertain. Also, we need to know the number of car kilometres travelled per year.

To arrive at an estimate for road space, the authors have multiplied the total 'road space' (the degraded land of the road network) for the UK by the percentage used by cars (86 per cent) and then divided by the total number of car-kilometres per year (362.4 billion).

Built land: 2,581,747 * 0.86 / 362,400,000,000 * 10,000 = 0.06
0.06 * 2.8 = 0.17 m^2 per car-km per year, where:

2,581,747 equals the area (in hectares) of the UK given over to roads based on conservative assumptions about carriageway width.
0.86 equals the proportion of roads that is used by private cars.[19]
362,400,000,000 is the total number of UK car km per year.[20]
10,000 converts hectares to m^2.
2.8 is the equivalence factor for built-upon land.

Adding the estimates for built land to energy land we get the car travel footprint:

= 0.73 + 0.17 = 0.90m² per car-kilometre per year.

To obtain some idea of the sensitivity of this figure, we further consider two other reported 'uplift' factors,[21] which go some way to providing high and low estimates (see Table 5.4). It can be seen that even considering these more extreme data, the final footprint figure remains fairly constant.

Table 5.4 *Footprint per Car-kilometre for Different Uplift Factors*

Estimate	Uplift factor (per cent)	Footprint per UK car-kilometre (m²)
Low	11	0.73
Medium	45	0.90
High	93	1.13

Table 5.5 *Ecological Footprint Estimates for Passenger Transport*[22]

Transport	Footprint (hectare years per 1000 passenger km)	Assumptions
Car	0.06 to 0.13	Based on petrol consumption, uplift for construction, maintenance and infrastructure, an estimate for apportioned road space and average passenger occupancy. Lower figure is based on EU data, the upper figure on US data
Bus and train	0.03	Assumes fuel consumption data (diesel) and embodied energy. Accounts for fuel and material energy and uses an assumption for apportioned road/rail space. On closer analysis buses usually have the advantage over trains
Air	0.06 to 0.09	Energy and degraded land are included for this estimate. With the current method no account has been taken for upper atmosphere emissions. Lower figure is based on long-haul flights (which are overall more energy efficient per km). The higher figure should be used for short-haul air travel.

Table 5.6 *Ecological Footprint Estimates for Freight Transport*

Freight	Footprint (hectare years per 1000 t-km)	Assumptions
Train	0.01	An estimate for a diesel freight train. Includes fuel, manufacture and maintenance energy plus an estimate of apportioned rail space (from EU data)
Road	0.07	Heavy goods vehicle (HGV) embodied energy per t-km with a proportioned area of the road network used by freight (from EU data)
Sea	0.01	The energy footprint of a coaster. This calculation does not include any sea or land areas associated with the freight movement (from EU data)
Air	0.32	The footprint estimate for air freight uses embodied energy and apportioned degraded land components (from EU data). No upper atmosphere emissions have been included.

FOOD

Food is the most basic requirement to sustain human existence, yet many, in industrialized countries especially, have become detached from the means and methods of food production, processing and distribution. This is not surprising given the low numbers now working the land. Farmers make up only 1 per cent of the US and 10 per cent of the EU population compared to 60 per cent of those in Africa.[23]

Intensive agriculture has not only concentrated food production in the hands of a few, it has also facilitated the global market in food. The palates of a population are no longer constrained by what can be grown within its local region. Meat, fruit and vegetables can, and often are, shipped or trucked halfway round the world before they land on the plates of hungry consumers. Thus the UK imports apples from New Zealand, the US, South Africa and continental Europe as well as producing its own varieties.

The ease with which produce can be traded globally has encouraged the development of monoculture, and even whole economies, geared towards the production of a narrow range of crops. For example, 70 per cent of the agricultural exports of the island of St Vincent in the

Retail   Bakery   Mills
(4.2)   (9.3)   (2.6)

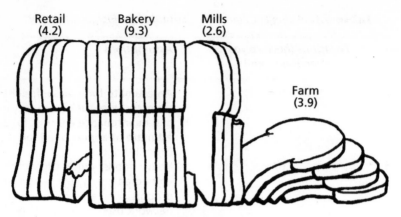

Farm
(3.9)

Figure 5.1 *Contribution to the fuel costs of a standard (20 slice) white loaf*

Caribbean are bananas, and the crop provides employment for half of the workforce.[24]

Two main environmental concerns have arisen from the transformation of food production into a global 'agribusiness'. First is the increasing use of artificial pesticides, herbicides, and fertilizers to increase yields and kill the pests and diseases that thrive in monoculture conditions. The second is the environmental impact of transporting foods over long distances – the so-called 'food miles'. The latter also necessitates additional packaging and treatment for the preservation and protection of the product in transit.

The energy required to grow, process and transport intensively-produced food often exceeds the energy contained within the food itself. The SAFE Alliance report that a standard 750 g white loaf of bread requires 5.6 kwh to produce – 2.5 times the food energy contained within the loaf.[25] A quarter of this energy goes on transport and packaging alone (see Figure 5.1).

As well as substantial inputs of energy, food production also requires direct land use for the growing of crops and the grazing of livestock. Trade in foodstuffs is usually considered in terms of its commercial value or tonnage, but by importing food one is also appropriating land in the producer country. Little data are kept on this aspect of trade but one study by FoE traced imports back to their countries of origin and worked out the yields for each of the main agricultural imports (excluding wood products). This showed that the UK is a net importer of more than four million hectares of land, which is used to supplement its own productive land area of about 17 million hectares.[26]

Table 5.7 outlines the footprint estimates presented by the authors for the main food types. In each case global average yields have been used, with allowances made for agricultural energy, processing and transportation based on mainly EU data.

Table 5.7 *Ecological Footprint Estimates for Various Foods*[27]

Food	Footprint (hectare years per tonne)	Assumptions
Grain	1.7 to 2.8	Average global yields are assumed and an allowance made for transport, processing and agriculture energy
Pulses	3.6 to 4.4	Average global yields are assumed and an allowance made for transport, processing and agriculture energy
Roots and Vegetables	0.3 to 0.6	The average global yields are reported as the average for the whole group, not a single crop example. An allowance is made for transport, processing and agriculture energy
Meat	6.9 to 14.6	This footprint estimate is calculated by using average global yield and embodied energy data. Range is due in the main to the different rearing methods. The lower estimate pertains to pasture-fed cattle, the upper to grain-fed animals.
Milk	1.1 to 1.9	Average global yields are assumed and an allowance made for transport, processing and agriculture energy.
Fish (pelagic)	4.5 to 6.6	Does not include aquaculture although studies have suggested that intensity of fish farming is countered by higher levels of resource use. This footprint estimate is produced from a global protein yield estimate and assuming the embodied energy is diesel.
Fruit	0.5 to 0.6	Average global yields are assumed and an allowance made for transport, processing and agriculture energy

cco perponior ad puts a figure to impact.

Box 5.5 Derivation Example – 'The Slippery Banana Footprint'

As an export crop, the banana has been well studied, being the fifth most important globally-traded commodity (worth US$7.5 billion in 1993). The main production areas are Latin America and India, with smaller producers in areas such as the Caribbean. In 1995 the International Institute for Environment and Development (IIED) undertook a footprint case study looking at bananas,[28] and established the following data:

UK consumption per person = 10 kg per year (1993)
5 kg per year (1983)
Average banana yield = 12 tonnes or 12,000 kg/ha per year[29]
1995 UK Population = 58,000,000

By dividing the UK per person consumption figure by the yield, an approximate UK banana footprint per person is obtained:

Productive land: 10/12000 = 8.3 m^2 per person.

This can then be translated into global average productive space by using the arable land equivalence factor.

Global average land: 8.3 * 2.8 = 23.2m^2 per person.

A simple banana footprint for the UK is calculated using the productive land only: 23.2 * 58,000,000 / 10,000 = c 134,500 ha,[30] where

23.2 = the annual per person footprint in m^2
58,000,000 = the UK population in 1995
10,000 = to convert from m^2 to ha

It is important to note here that this is a simple, baseline footprint and does not account for other impacts such as transportation and other energy inputs into the production and distribution process.

MATERIALS AND WASTE

Despite trends in recycling and reuse, the use of virgin materials has continued its inexorable rise. Today more than 1.6 tonnes of raw materials (minerals, metals, wood and synthetics) are produced or extracted per person per year (see Figure 5.2). This is equivalent to an average four kilogrammes per day, with people in the industrialized world using far larger amounts.

Americans are the 'king' consumers with a daily load of 101 kg – the weight of a large man – equivalent to 37 tonnes per annum, 25 times the global average.[31] In comparison, a mass–balance study of the UK revealed a daily load of 27 kg – the weight of a small child – equiva-

Source: Worldwatch Institute (1998) (See note 34)

Figure 5.2 *Total world materials production (1963–1995)*

lent to 10 tonnes per annum.[32] Even allowing for the problematic calculations involved in reaching these figures, volumes such as these are hard to acknowledge without reference to the hidden 'ecological rucksacks' that are attached to the manufactured goods we consume.[33] A metal item, for example, requires the mining of ore many times its own finished weight. More than 95 per cent of the ore mined in the production of copper, gold, zinc, lead, nickel, tin and tungsten becomes waste.[34] This excludes the 'overburden' – the amount of material removed to gain access to the ore. Other metals fare little better.

Such volumes dwarf the tonnage of domestic waste produced – often the only visible sign of a wasteful lifestyle. Canada's mining wastes, for example, are 58 times greater that its urban refuse.[35]

The environmental impact of materials use arises from two main sources: the direct effects of the extraction and the energy used in mining and processing the ore. Resource depletion is a controversial issue to try and quantify. Firstly, it is difficult to predict abundance, and secondly, the availability is related to the economics of extraction. For example, the relatively new technique of in situ leaching could affect the economics of copper and uranium mining.[36]

Table 5.8 *Abundance of Various Elements*[37]

Elements (order from least to most abundant)	Average crust abundance (per cent)
Gold	0.00000035
Silver	0.0000075
Mercury	0.0000089
Tin	0.00017
Lead	0.0012
Chromium	0.0011
Copper	0.0063
Titanium	0.64
Iron	5.82
Aluminium	8.3

Best guesses on abundance (see Table 5.8) show that some materials such as iron and aluminium are effectively unlimited in that they make up 5.8 per cent and 8.3 per cent of the earth's crust whereas reserves of gold, silver and mercury are far less abundant.

Although energy use is related to ore concentration for a particular material, it is also the case that some materials are inherently far more energy-intensive to produce than others. Thus aluminium, an abundant substance, also has one of the highest embodied energies, requiring between 210–374 MJ per kg.[38] Aluminium smelting accounts for around one per cent of all world energy use.

Turning to the direct land use involved in materials extraction, there is both intentional and unintentional land degradation resulting from mining.[39] Examples include:

- Pollution from the Norilsk nickel plant in Russia destroyed 300,000 ha of forest.
- The local Wopkamin peoples of New Guinea lost 7000 ha of land to gold and copper mining.
- 2000 ha of the Doñana National Park in Spain was seriously affected by mining sludge.
- Mining of titanium oxide in Madagascar will destroy at least 6280 ha of forest.

Many of the factors that have already been highlighted – mining technology, ore concentration and nature of the material being extracted – complicate measurement of direct land use. When calculating an ecological footprint for materials, it is often the case that direct land use is ignored in favour of using embodied energy as a proxy for the full set of impacts. In this text we have made an allowance for direct land use, but accept that more work needs to be done to measure this more accurately for selected materials.

Box 5.6 Derivation Example – 'The Footprint News'[40]

As an example, let us consider the footprint of a broadsheet newspaper containing 80 per cent recycled material and 20 per cent virgin material.

Step One – Calculating the Footprint for a Tonne of Virgin Paper

The World Energy Council reports that processing paper requires 25 GJ per tonne. Assuming that the newspaper is produced in the EU and the energy is derived from grid electricity, this figure can then be translated to CO_2 emissions and the land needed for sequestration.

Energy (process) land: 25 * 0.2 * 0.19 = 0.96,
0.96 * 1.17 = 1.12 hectare years per tonne of virgin paper, where:

25 is the energy used in gigajoules per tonne of virgin paper
0.2 equals the tonnes of CO_2 produced per gigajoule of EU electricity
0.19 is the area (in hectares) needed to sequester a tonne of CO_2
1.17 is the energy land equivalence factor

The second input to produce our 'Footprint News' is the transport energy. The Paper Industry Research Association reports the CO_2 emissions from transportation to be 69.3 kg CO_2 per tonne. Again, this can be translated to CO_2 sequestration land.

Energy (transport) land: 69.3 * 0.00019 = 0.013
0.013 * 1.17 = 0.015 ha years per tonne of virgin paper, where:

69.3 is the amount of CO_2, in kg produced per tonne of virgin paper
0.00019 equals the area (ha) of land needed to sequester a kilogram of CO_2
1.17 is the energy land equivalence factor

The final input, and simplest to express, is the direct land use required for 'Footprint News' wood. Here we use a world average yield of 1.99 m³ per ha per year. A tonne of paper requires 1.8 m³ of wood and so dividing this by the yield gives us a hectarage per tonne of virgin paper;

Productive land: 1.8/1.99 = 0.91
0.91 * 1.17 = 1.06 ha years per tonne of virgin paper, where:

1.8 is the volume (m³) of wood required for a tonne of virgin paper
1.99 is the volume (m³) of wood produced per hectare in the northern hemisphere
1.17 is the forest land equivalence factor

The virgin component of the newspaper can now be calculated – ecological footprint: 1.06 + 1.12 + 0.015 = 2.2 ha years per tonne virgin paper.
    A single edition of the 'Footprint News' weighs an estimated 200 g. Now we can calculate the footprint of the virgin component only:

Ecological footprint: 2.2 / 1000 * 0.2 * 0.2 * 10,000 = 0.88 m² for a year per newspaper, where:

2.2 is divided by 1000 to get ha per kg of virgin paper
multiplied by 0.2 to obtain the ha per 200g of virgin paper
and then multiplied by 0.2 again to derive the 20 per cent virgin paper figure. To convert ha to m², this is then multiplied by 10,000.

Step Two – Calculating the Footprint for a Tonne of Recycled Paper

The recycled component, 80 per cent of the newspaper, is accounted for here by the energy saved by using recycled compared to virgin paper. Hence, no forest land is required and less process energy is needed. Yet, in the estimate we present, no account is taken for transportation, which is likely to be significant in the UK due to the distances between recycling facilities and manufacturers. For example, Aylesford Newsprint state that the average journey for collection and delivery of waste paper is 11.5 km.

Firstly, the embodied energy of virgin paper was calculated by using the figures stated above for processing and transportation. This resulted in a figure of 7.24 kWh per kg of virgin paper. Once this was established, the embodied energy figure was multiplied by the recycled paper 'energy saving factor'. According to FoE, recycled paper uses only 30 per cent of the energy required for virgin paper production. Therefore:

Energy land: 7.24 * 0.3 * 0.00049 * 0.19 = 0.0002
0.0002 * 1.17 = 0.00023 ha per kg recycled paper per year, where:

7.24 is the embodied energy of virgin paper, in kWh per kg
0.3 is the amount of energy recycled paper uses compared to virgin paper
0.00049 is the tonnes of CO_2 produced per kWh of UK electricity in a particular year
0.19 equals the land area in hectares needed to sequester a tonne of CO_2 per year
1.17 is the energy land equivalence factor

Now, we can calculate the footprint of the recycled component of 'Footprint News'.

Ecological footprint: 0.00023 * 0.2 * 0.8 * 10,000 = 0.37 m² per newspaper per year where:
0.2 converts the ha per kg, to a ha per 200 g (the weight of a broadsheet newspaper)
0.8 represents the 80 per cent of the newspaper made of recycled paper
10,000 converts ha to m²

Step Three – Calculating the Footprint Newspaper

Finally we can now add the two hectare figures to get the footprint of a broadsheet newspaper containing 80 per cent recycled material. It is

0.88 + 0.37 = 1.25 m² years per newspaper.

Table 5.9 *Ecological Footprint Estimate for Various Materials and Waste*[41]

Materials and waste	Footprint (hectare years per tonne)	Assumptions
Timber	1.0 to 5.7	Estimate based on weight of usable construction timber. Includes growing land plus embodied energy for processing and transportation. Lower end of range relates to softwoods. Upper end of range to be used for hardwoods
Concrete	0.1	Uses the embodied energy of the finished product plus an estimate of degraded land caused by mining of aggregates
Steel	0.8 to 1.4	High energy use in the production of steel accounts for a vast part of the footprint. A degraded land estimate has been added to account for mining of the resources
Cotton garments	5.6 to 5.8	This estimate uses the global cotton yield, which can vary immensely. Also included is the energy required to manufacture a finished garment
Paper – landfilled	2.8 to 4.0	Accounted for through the embodied energy and materials in the waste plus an allowance for the landfill impact
Paper – recycled	2.0 to 2.9	Calculated by the energy 'saved' by recycling compared to virgin production
Glass – landfilled	1.0 to 1.1	Embodied energy of a virgin product, plus the landfill land
Glass – recycled	0.8 to 0.9	Based on energy savings derived from recycling glass
Aluminium cans – landfilled	9.4 to 17.8	The estimate here accounts for embodied energy, mining land and landfill land. High embodied energy content of average aluminium accounts for the vast majority of the estimate. The upper end of the range is primary aluminium
Aluminium cans – recycled	0.4 to 0.9	Accounted by the energy savings compared to virgin production. Savings occur through the reduced need for primary aluminium
Plastic – landfilled	3.6 to 4.1	Embodied energy and landfill land. Embodied energy estimates are based on nine different plastics
Plastic – recycled	1.1 to 3.3	Energy savings through recycling. The recycling of plastic is more complex and benefits harder to determine without specific data. The energy savings used for this estimate reach just over 20 per cent. Range of data reflects different levels of energy savings possible with recycling/reuse

Note: based on deliverable/usable tonnages

Calculating an ecological footprint for renewable materials, primarily forestry products, is much more transparent, being based on more readily available yield and processing data.

Of course, waste is merely another name for unwanted materials. What counts as disposable varies from country to country. More than 90 per cent of bottles are reused or recycled in Denmark,[42] compared with 27 per cent in the UK (on average over 50 per cent of bottles are recycled in Europe).[43]

Material flows through the economy can be measured as they enter or exit the system. Such analyses can also be done, given data availability, at a number of different levels. For example, much interesting work is being done on the organizational metabolism of materials.[44] A simple way of dealing with waste at the local level is to consider the contents of the waste stream – what is recycled and what is sent for disposal. This is the approach we take here, although it is certainly more accurate to measure overall flows where such data are available (see the later examples of national footprints).

The footprint conversion factors for a selection of material and waste types are given in Table 5.9.

WATER

Water is constantly circulating through our ecosystems – a process known as the hydrological cycle. The total amount of water on our planet is truly vast, estimated at 1.4 x 1018 m^3. Most of this is salt water. Of the fresh water, much is locked up in the polar ice caps. Only 1015 m^3 of fresh water (0.07 per cent of the total) is available for our use. Most of this is present as groundwater – underground water reserves. These supplies are unevenly distributed around the globe – some areas are blessed with ample amounts whilst others find it difficult to obtain drinking water of sufficient quality. As a result close to 20 per cent of the global population, around 1.3 billion people, lack access to safe water.[45] Table 5.10 shows the percentage of people without access to safe water. The issue of water pollution is not restricted to the poorer regions of the world. Nitrates above the EU permissible limits contaminate almost a quarter of the groundwater in Europe. This is mainly the result of high levels of fertilizer use. The EU is now proposing legislation to filter drinking water that will require the use of energy intensive membrane technologies to achieve acceptable levels.

Water is a highly regional resource that is rarely transported long distances because of its bulk and hence relatively high cost. However, water-intensive products are often transported long distances because of their added value. For example, orange juice, cotton and wine all have high levels of 'embodied' water. Often these are exported from countries or regions that can ill afford to lose the precious liquid. One-third of the global population live in countries experiencing moderate to high water stress. World Resources (1998–99) report water as a 'resource at risk', adding that 'The world's thirst for water is likely to become one of the most pressing resource issues of the 21st century'.[46] The report goes on to point out that water use has outstripped population growth by a factor of two. Worldwide, most water (about 70 per cent) is used for agriculture, followed by industrial and then domestic usage (see Figure 5.3).

Published data indicate that at the continental level, North America and Europe have few water problems. Europe as a whole withdraws just 7 per cent of its water resource, North America just 10 per cent. Yet these figures mask considerable variations: Germany draws on 48 per cent of its renewable reserves, Bulgaria 77 per cent, and Hungary 117 per cent. Any region over 20 per cent is considered to have 'moderate' water stress.

When footprinting water use (Table 5.11) we consider only the embodied energy (see the derivation example in Box 5.7). This is arguably the most generally applicable method and that which is least subject to regional variation. However, where countries are experiencing high levels of water stress, or where agricultural run-off is leading to local pollution, it is appropriate to consider a broader set of ecological impacts (see Box 5.8, which looks at the calculation of water catchment areas).

Table 5.10 *Lack of Access to Safe Water
a Regional Profile (1990–96)*

Region	Percentage without access to safe water
Arab States	21
sub-Saharan Africa	48
South-East Asia and the Pacific	35
Latin America and the Caribbean	23
East Asia	32
East Asia (excluding China)	13
South Asia	18
'Developing' countries	29
'Least developed' countries	43

Source: Human Development Report (1998) (see note 45)

LIVERPOOL
JOHN MOORES UNIVERSITY
AVRIL ROBARTS LRC
TITHEBARN STREET
LIVERPOOL L2 2ER
TEL. 0151 231 4022

Table 5.11 *Footprint Calculations for Water*[47]

Water use	Unit	Footprint (m²-years)	Assumptions
Cold tap water	per 100 litres	0.08	Based on data from a UK water company. Accounts only for the embodied energy for the supply of water
Washing machine	per 100 washes	255	Based on data from several UK water companies. Accounts for the embodied energy of the water. Electricity is assumed to be used to heat the water
Dishwasher	per 100 washes	167	Based on data from several UK water companies. Accounts for the embodied energy of the water. Electricity is assumed to be used to heat the water
Bath	per 100 baths	98	Based on data from several UK water companies. Accounts for the embodied energy of the water. Electricity is assumed to be used to heat the water
Shower	per 100 showers	27	Based on data from several UK water companies. Accounts for the embodied energy of the water. Electricity is assumed to be used to heat the water.
Toilet	per 100 flushes	1.24	Based on data from a UK water company. Accounts only for the embodied energy for the supply of water

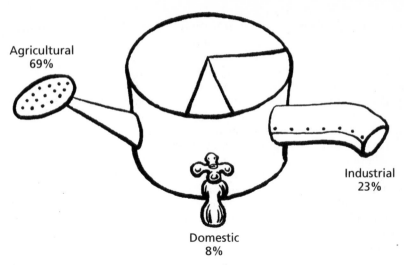

Agricultural
69%

Industrial
23%

Domestic
8%

Source: World Resources (1998–99) (see note 46)

Figure 5.3 *Water withdrawals by sector (1987)*

Box 5.7 Derivation Example (Method 1) – 'Walking on Water'

For calculating the footprint of water we conservatively account only for the energy needed to treat, pipe, supply and, where applicable, heat the water. Data provided by a UK utilities company show that each megalitre (1 million litres) of water delivered results in the emission of around 370kg of CO_2.

The ecological footprint for a megalitre can then be derived by dividing the CO_2 figure by applying the footprint value for CO_2

Ecological footprint = 370 * 0.00019 * 1.17 = 0.08 ha years, where:
0.00019 is the area needed to sequester one kilogramme of CO_2
1.17 is the equivalence factor for forest land.

This method may lead to double counting of energy when this is already included in a regional calculation. However, for calculating the footprint of a small region, organization or household, this method can be used.

In some instances it is also interesting to find out how much area is necessary to 'catch' the water. Such catchment areas do not usually form part of the overall footprint calculation to avoid double counting. For this reason the authors refer to it as a 'shadow footprint' (see Box 5.8).

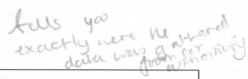

tells you exactly here he attered data was gathered from for authority

---

Box 5.8 Derivation Example (Method 2) – The 'Shadow Footprint' of Water

The second method of calculating water footprints is by using catchment areas.[48] This reflects the water resource available, from whatever source, of an 'average' hectare of land within a particular region. The World Resource figures for Germany and Saudi Arabia, for example, show that they have 96 and 2.4 km^3 of internal renewable water resources and land areas of 34.9 million and 214.9 million ha respectively.

We refer to the water catchment footprint as a 'shadow' footprint since, unlike footprints for other resources and wastes, it is not additive. Most land types also serve a water catchment function.

The shadow footprint for a country can be calculated by dividing the land area by the renewable water resource.[49] To this must be added any energy required to treat and distribute the water (as in the earlier example).

Looking solely at catchment areas, we present the calculations for two countries:

1 Germany
   34.9 million ha / 96,000 million m^3 = 0.36 ha per Ml per year
2 Saudi Arabia
   214.9 million ha / 2400 million m^3 = 89.57 ha per Ml per year

Expressed another way, an average hectare of German land has the potential to supply 2748 m^3 of water, enough at the current German consumption rate for about five persons. By comparison, an average hectare of Saudi Arabia's land has the potential to supply 11 m^3, which is less than one-tenth of one person's water consumption. Switching to desalinization plants is one option for water-poor regions but this massively increases the amount of energy required to process supplies.

QUESTIONS

- Why have some footprint numbers gone up? (see Chapter 6, Question 8)
- We are using up many of our material resources such as copper and tin. How does ecological footprinting measure this resource depletion? (see Chapter 6, Question 12)
- How does ecological footprinting deal with pollution such as SO_2 (responsible for acid rain)? (see Chapter 6, Question 14)
- A big part of any footprint appears to be due to energy use. If we switch to energy sources that do not add CO_2 to the atmosphere, such as solar energy, won't this dramatically reduce our footprint to the point that the concept is meaningless? (see Chapter 6, Question 18)
- What about nuclear power? (see Chapter 6, Question 19)

Box 5.9 Health Warning – The Double-Counting Demon

The twist at the end of all these tables and calculations is the demon of double counting, which always rears its ugly head when adding up component footprints at a regional level (there is no danger of this happening when looking at individual organizations, products or lifestyle or when working with compound footprints which are based on resource flows rather than activities).

If you are not careful then your footprint result will be inflated by the double counting of impacts. For example, the energy used by business and industry in producing goods for consumption could – if you are not vigilant – be counted both in your energy and materials footprints.

The authors' experience is that double-counting issues are most significant for energy, freight transport and materials and waste. Two simple rules should prevent you falling prey to this demon:

- It is recommended that you remove all energy used by industry to counter that already accounted for within the individual consumption of goods and services.
- To help eliminate the demon from the travel components, it is recommended that you subtract the road freight footprint from your overall result. This may be an over-precaution, but many of its elements will already be accounted for by the embodied energy within consumer goods and the road space will be included within the built land figures.

NOTES

1   Climate trends paint a convincing picture of human-induced change. Global temperature fluctuations neatly match atmospheric concentrations of carbon dioxide. For example, see the work being done by the Global Commons Institute: www.gci.org.uk (last accessed 25/11/99)

2   1 tonne of oil equivalent is equal to 41.87 Gigjoules (GJ)

3   Gipe, 1999, 'How much energy does it take to build a wind system in relation to the energy it produces?' from *Wind Energy Weekly*. Taken from the American Wind Energy Association web site http://www.awea.org/faq/bal.html, accessed 30/03/99

4   Stelzer, T and Wiese, A, 1994, 'Ganzheitliche Bilanzierung der Stromerzevgung aus erneuerbaren Energieträgem, 9' in FoE Europe, 1995

5   Estimated in *Our Ecological Footprint*, 1996, Wackernagel, M and Rees, W, New Society Publishers, Gabriola Island, BC, p107

6   Stelzer, T and Wiese, A, 1994, op cit

7   American Wind Energy Association, 1999, 'How much land is required for large wind plants?', http://www.awea.org/faq/land.html, accessed on 30/03/99. This source states that the area of degraded land apportioned for a wind farm is actually 12 hectares per GWh. However, they later state that 5 per cent of this area is directly occupied by the wind turbines. The 5 per cent of the 12 hectares gives us our 0.6 hectares per GWh estimate which we use here

8   See *Energy Policy in the Greenhouse: From warming fate to warming limit*, by
     Krause, F, Bach, W and Koomey, J, Earthscan Publications, London,
     1990, p44. IPCC estimate similar figures – see earlier
9   See, for example, 'Bogging down in the Sinks' by Ashley Mattoon,
     Worldwatch Magazine, November/December 1998; *Buenos Aires Post-
     Mortem* by Christopher Flavin, November 1998, Worldwatch Institute.
     Both articles available on the internet at the Worldwatch site
     http://www.worldwatch.org, last accessed 25/11/99
10   Comparing the world as perceived by a traveller based on an average
     speed of 25km/h or 15mph (that achieved by the fictional character
     Phileas Fogg in *Around the World in 80 Days*) and the size of the world as
     perceived by a passenger able to achieve an average speed of 500km/h or
     300mph (easily achievable by modern air transport)
11   Sources for Tables 5.2 and 5.3: Intergovernmental Panel on Climate
     Change, 1996, *Greenhouse Gas Inventory. Revised guidelines for National
     Greenhouse Gas Inventories*, IPCC Secretariat, c/o World Meteorological
     Organisation, Geneva, Switzerland; Wackernagel, M, Lewan, L, and
     Borgström-Hansson, C, 1999, 'Evaluating the use of natural capital with
     the ecological footprint: Applications in Sweden and subregions', *Ambio*,
     vol 28, no 7, Nov 1999, pp604–612; Mathis Wackernagel, Larry Onisto,
     Patricia Bello, Alejandro Callejas Linares, Ina Susana López Falfán, Jesus
     Méndez García, Ana Isabel Suárez Guerrero, Ma. Guadalupe Suárez
     Guerrero, 1999, 'National natural capital accounting with the ecological
     footprint concept', *Ecological Economics* 29, pp375–390; Ekvall, T, Person,
     L, Ryberg, A, Widheden, J, Frees, N, Nielsen, Per H, Pedersen, BW and
     Wesnaes, M, 1998, *Life Cycle Assessment of Packaging Systems for Beer and
     Soft Drinks*. Miljøprojekt nr 399, Danish Environmental Protection
     Agency, Ministry of Environment and Energy, Denmark; International
     Energy Agency, 1998, *Key Energy Statistics*. http://www.iea.org;
     Department of Trade and Industry, 1997, *Digest of United Kingdom Energy
     Statistics 1997*, Government Statistical Service, London; Gipe, P, 1999,
     *How much energy does it take to build a wind system in relation to the energy
     it produces?*, downloaded 30/03/99 from *Wind Energy Weekly*,
     http://www.awea.org /faq/bal.html; American Wind Energy Association,
     1999, *How much land is required for large wind plants?*, downloaded
     30/03/99 from *Wind Energy Weekly*, http://www.awea.org/faq/bal.html;
     Alsema, EA, Frankl, P and Kato, K, 1998, *Energy Pay-Back Time of
     Photovoltaic Energy Systems: Present status and prospects*, presented at the
     2nd World Conference on Photovoltaic Solar Energy Conversion,
     Vienna, 6–10 July 1998 (Report No 98053); Alsema, EA, 1996,
     Environmental Aspects of Solar Cell Modules – Summary Report, Report No
     96074, Utrecht University, The Netherlands; Krotscheck, C and
     Narodoslawsky, M, 1996, 'The Sustainable Process index: A new dimen-
     sion in ecological evaluation', *Ecological Engineering*, vol 6, no 4,
     pp241–258; Stelzer, T and Wiese, A, 1994, 'Ganzheitliche Bilanzierung
     der Stromerzeugung aus erneuerbaren Energietragern, 9', in Friends of
     the Earth Europe, 1995, *Towards Sustainable Europe*, Friends of the Earth
     Netherlands, Amsterdam
12   About 22.6 tonnes of fuel is used per hour of flying. A conservative
     estimate of 70 tonnes of fuel is required for the trip, or 700kg per
     passenger. Assuming each passenger weighs 70kg, then fuel use is 10

times their own body weight – return trip is therefore 20 times their own body weight. Calculated from data contained within Unofficial Concorde Homepage: http://www.geocities.com/CapeCanaveral/Lab/8952/0fre_tech.htm

13 See Transport Statistics Great Britain, 1997 Edition, p8
14 *State of the World 1998*, Lester R Brown et al, 1998, p115, Worldwatch Institute/Earthscan, London
15 Authors' own calculations. Assumes 6-lane motorway with 3-metre lanes plus 2 'hard shoulder' lanes and 2-metre barrier. Total width of 26 metres. So each kilometre (1000 metres) of road requires at least 2.6 hectares. This is most likely a conservative estimate. Based on the figures given by Professor John Whitelegg (in *Critical Mass*, Pluto Press, 1997), the effective width of the Birmingham North Relief Road works out to 130 metres!
16 Estimated in Wackernagel and Rees, 1996, *Our Ecological Footprint*, New Society Publishers
17 See *EU Transport in Figures: Statistical Pocket Book 1998*, updated January 1999, Eurostat, Luxembourg
18 See the UK Department of the Environment, Transport and the Regions (DETR), 1997, *Transport Statistics Great Britain 1997 Edition*, Government Statistical Service, London, p36
19 See DETR, 1997, *Transport Statistics Great Britain 1997 Edition*, Government Statistical Service, London, p8
20 See British Road Federation, 1998, 'Road Fact 98' leaflet (1996 data)
21 11 per cent based on manufacturing energy, source: Hill, R, O'Keefe, P and Snape, C, 1995, *Future of Energy Use*, Earthscan/Worldwatch publication, p18. 93 per cent based on life cycle study by Teufel et al, 1993, quoted in Whitelegg, 1997, *Critical Mass*, Pluto Press, p29
22 Sources for Tables 5.5 and 5.6: Department of the Environment, Transport and the Regions, 1997, *Transport Statistics Great Britain*, Government Statistical Service, London; Wackernagel, M, Lewan, L, and Borgström-Hansson, C, 1999, 'Evaluating the use of natural capital with the ecological footprint: Applications in Sweden and subregions', *Ambio*, vol 28, no 7, Nov 1999, pp604–612; Eurostat 1999, *EU Transport in Figures: Statistical pocket book* (Updated January 1999); British Road Federation, 1998, *Road Facts 98*; DETR, 1999, personal communication, National Travel Survey; Whitelegg, J, 1994, *Transport for a Sustainable Future: The case for Europe*, J Wiley & Son, Chichester; Railtrack, 1999, personal communication; Ekvall, T, Person, L, Ryberg, A, Widheden, J, Frees, N, Nielsen, Per H, Pedersen, BW and Wesnaes, M, 1998, *Life Cycle Assessment of Packaging Systems for Beer and Soft Drinks*. Miljøprojekt nr 399, Danish Environmental Protection Agency, Ministry of Environment and Energy, Denmark; Whitelegg, J, 1997, *Critical Mass: Transport, Environment and Society in the Twenty-first Century*, London, Pluto Press
23 'Letting the World Feed Itself', published by Friedrich Wilhelm Graefe zu Baringdorf (MEP) and Hannes Lorenzen, Green Group in the European Parliament, 1997
24 'On the banana front line', *The Sunday Telegraph*, March 14th 1999, p25
25 'The Food Miles Report: The dangers of long distance food transport' 1994, produced by Angela Paxton for the SAFE Alliance
26 McLaren, D, Bullock, S and Yousuf, N, 1998, *Tomorrow's World*, Earthscan, London, p14

27   Data sources for Table 5.7: FAO web site, http://www.fao.org (accessed in 1999); Wackernagel, M, Lewan, L, and Borgström-Hansson, C, 1999, 'Evaluating the use of natural capital with the ecological footprint: Applications in Sweden and subregions' *Ambio*, vol 28, no 7, Nov 1999, pp604–612; Whitelegg, J, 1994, *Transport for a Sustainable Future: The case for Europe*, J Wiley & Son, Chichester; Mathis Wackernagel, Larry Onisto, Patricia Bello, Alejandro Callejas Linares, Ina Susana López Falfán, Jesus Méndez García, Ana Isabel Suárez Guerrero, Ma. Guadalupe Suárez Guerrero, 1999, 'National natural capital accounting with the ecological footprint concept', *Ecological Economics*, vol 29, pp375–390; MAFF, 1997, *National Food Survey 1997: Annual report on Food Expenditure, Consumption and Nutrient Intakes*, Government Statistical Service, London; MAFF, 1997, *UK Food and Farming in Figures*, Government Statistical Service, London; Department of Trade and Industry, 1999, *Digest of United Kingdom Energy Statistics*, Government Statistical Service, London; Department of Trade and Industry, 1997, *Digest of United Kingdom Energy Statistics*, Government Statistical Service, London

28   IIED, 1995, *Citizen Action to Lighten Britain's Ecological Footprints*, IIED, London

29   Exporter markets to the UK are The Windward Isles, Guatemala, Jamaica, Honduras, Belize, Colombia, Suriname, Ecuador, Costa Rica, Cameroon

30   The unadjusted figure (before applying the equivalence factor) is close to the data reported in McLaren, Bullock and Yousuf, op cit, of 53,000 hectares (based on 1995 data)

31   Gardner, G and Sampat, P, 1998, 'Mind over Matter: Recasting the role of materials in our lives', Worldwatch Paper 144, December 1998

32   'Great Britain Plc', October 1997, Biffa Waste Services, High Wycombe, UK. The difference between the UK and US consumption figures is just as likely to reflect differences in study methodology as any real differences in consumption

33   As an example, McLaren, Bullock and Yousef quote that 1 tonne of aluminium produces 50 tonnes of waste, McLaren, Bullock and Yousef, 1998, op cit. Figures from the Worldwatch Institute suggest that 'only' 70 per cent of the ore becomes waste perhaps because the latter does not include the 'overburden', the material removed to reach the ore

34   Gardner, G and Sampat, P, 1998, 'Mind over Matter: Recasting the role of materials in our lives', Worldwatch Paper 144, December 1998, pp18 and 19

35   See von Weizsäcker, 1998, 'Dematerialisation: why and how?' in *Managing a Material World*, Kluwer Academic Publishers, Dordrecht, The Netherlands, and *Resource Flows: The material basis of industrial economies*, World Resources Institute, 1997

36   See the web site of FoE Australia for a discussion of the controversial technique of in situ leaching

37   Source: Meadows, Meadows and Randers, *Beyond the Limits*, 1992, Earthscan, London, p85

38   ETSU report B/W5/00337/REP 'Modelling of Carbon and Energy Budgets of Wood Fuel Coppice Systems', 1994

39   Worldwatch Institute, *State of the World 1999*, pp47–48, Earthscan and Friends of the Earth 'What's At Stake?', www.foe.co.uk/camps/biohab/, last accessed 17th March 1999

40   World Energy Council and PIRA data from *Towards a sustainable paper cycle*, IIED, 1996; Wackernagel, M, Lewan, L, and Borgström-Hansson, C, 1999, 'Evaluating the use of natural capital with the ecological footprint: Applications in Sweden and subregions', *Ambio*, vol 28, no 7, Nov 1999, pp604–612; Wackernagel M, and Rees WE, 1996, *Our Ecological Footprint*, New Society Publishers; Aylesford Newsprint, 1995, *Environmental Report*, Aylesford, Kent, UK; Friends of the Earth, 1991, *Recycling Officers' Handbook*, FoE (England and Wales), 1991

41   Data sources for Table 8.9: ETSU, 1994, Report B/W5/00337/REP *Modelling of Carbon and Energy Budgets of Wood Fuel Coppice Systems*; Wackernagel, M, Lewan, L, and Borgström-Hansson, C, 1999, 'Evaluating the use of natural capital with the ecological footprint: Applications in Sweden and subregions', *Ambio*, vol 28, no 7, Nov 1999, pp604–612; Mathis Wackernagel, Larry Onisto, Patricia Bello, Alejandro Callejas Linares, Ina Susana López Falfán, Jesus Méndez García, Ana Isabel Suárez Guerrero, Ma. Guadalupe Suárez Guerrero, 1999, 'National natural capital accounting with the ecological footprint concept', *Ecological Economics*, vol 29, pp375–390; Ekvall, T, Person, L, Ryberg, A, Widheden, J, Frees, N, Nielsen, Per H, Pedersen, BW and Wesnaes, M, 1998, *Life Cycle Assessment of Packaging Systems for Beer and Soft Drinks*, Miljøprojekt nr 399, Danish Environmental Protection Agency, Ministry of Environment and Energy, Denmark; Mathis Wackernagel, Larry Onisto, Alejandro Callejas Linares, Ina Susana López Falfán, Jesus Méndez García, Ana Isabel Suárez Guerrero, Ma. Guadalupe Suárez Guerrero, 1997, *Ecological Footprints of Nations: How Much Nature Do They Use? How Much Nature Do They Have?* Commissioned by ICLEI. Available on the internet via http://www.ecologicalfootprint.com; IIED, 1996, *Towards a sustainable paper cycle*, IIED; Friends of the Earth, *Recycling Officers' Handbook*, FoE (England and Wales), 1991; Boustead, I, 1993, 1994, 1995, 1996, 1997, 1998, 1999, *Eco-Balance methodology for Commodity Thermoplastics* and *Eco-Profiles of the European Plastics Industry* report series; Association of Plastics Manufacturers in Europe; Department of Trade and Industry, 1997, *Digest of United Kingdom Energy Statistics*, Government Statistical Service, London

42   Ekvall, T, Person, L, Ryberg, A, Widheden, J, Frees, N, Nielsen, Per H, Pedersen, B Weidma and Wesnoes, M, 1998, 'Life Cycle Assessment of Packaging Systems for Beer and Soft Drinks – Main Report', Miljøprojekt nr 399, Danish Environmental Protection Agency, Ministry of Environment and Energy, Denmark

43   Both the UK and European figures are available from British Glass: http://www.britglass.co uk/recycling

44   See, for example, the tools being developed by Natural Logic, http://www.natlogic.com

45   *Human Development Report 1998*, UNDP, OUP, Oxford

46   *World Resources 1998–99*, p188, WRI, OUP, Oxford

47   DTI, 1997, *Digest of United Kingdom Energy Statistics*, Government Statistical Office, London

48   This has previously been calculated for some Australian cities. See website: http://www.dwe.csiro.au/local/research/futures/pictures by Kalma, J D and Fleming, M, 1994

49   These data are available from *World Resources 1998–99*, op cit. Note: 1 cubic metre = 1000 litres.

Chapter 6

Twenty Questions about Ecological Footprinting

Over the years, the authors have learned most from the many questions, suggestions and often brilliant ideas arising from debate and discussion with colleagues and other interested parties. Who has used this method? Who has failed with footprints and why? What are its benefits? Could this concept be dangerous or could it be misused? What if corporations try to take it over? What is the footprint of my dog?

The list of ideas and suggestions is extensive and continues to grow.[1] Below we address what we perceive to be the main recurring themes in a question and answer format. These are cross-referenced from earlier sections in this book.

QUESTION 1– WHAT IS THE ADVANTAGE OF AGGREGATING DIFFERENT ENVIRONMENTAL IMPACTS INTO ONE INDICATOR?

With an aggregate indicator, such as the ecological footprint, it is easier to explore the connection between various ecological functions and how the various pressures on nature, such as biodiversity loss, erosion, water scarcity, CO_2 accumulation, interact. The authors have dubbed this the 'small bed-cover effect'. When one has a cold head at night the tendency is to pull the bed-cover over one's face. But then the feet start to stick out and get chilly. Similarly, once the footprint gets bigger than the ecological capacity, human uses compete against each other for ecological space. Alleviating the pressure on one ecosystem merely shifts the strain to another. For example, the increase in fish farming to overcome the depletion of the ocean fish stocks in turn requires more sea space for low grade fish and arable land for feed production. Or, worse, one impact may start to exacerbate another one. For example, deforestation decreases an area's humidity and therefore the productivity of surrounding ecosystems.

QUESTION 2 – ISN'T THE FOOTPRINT JUST ANOTHER ARBITRARY SUSTAINABILITY INDEX?

Far from it. The ecological footprint is based on the measurement of nature's interest – the resources that nature can renewably generate and the pollution that it can cope with. EFA recognizes the finite capacity of the planet and gives a clear indication of the amount of nature that we have and how much we are currently using. The footprint is also consistent with basic laws of thermodynamics (see Annexe 1: A Primer on Thermodynamics).

QUESTION 3 – ISN'T THE FOOTPRINT A BIT TOO SIMPLISTIC?

For sure, it would be ideal to model the total complexities of the world's ecological systems, but this is not possible and not necessary for most purposes. The ecological footprint is certainly one of the simpler models that describe human use of nature but one which serves a well defined purpose. Essentially, the ecological footprint is a planning tool to help people understand and deal more effectively with ecological limits. To be an effective planning tool, it is not necessary to have a sophisticated model of how nature works, but rather one which is easy to grasp. In this respect it acts as a 'least common denominator' model of nature's function.

QUESTION 4 – WHAT'S THE ADVANTAGE OF SIMPLIFYING SO MUCH?

Such a model encourages a more productive communication between opposing world views. In the authors' experience the simple premises behind the ecological footprint are accepted by a wide variety of people and thus provide a good common starting point for debate. It speaks to those who believe in human dependence on nature and the necessity to preserve ecological capacities to secure human survival. It also resonates with those who believe that economic activities are the origin of wealth and that only continued economic growth can ensure social peace. In other words, the footprint is a communal gathering point to encourage a diversity of people on a shared journey. Also, although the concept and representation of the footprint is essentially simplistic, the method and calculations used to derive those footprints can be as detailed as the data and human endeavour allow it to be.

QUESTION 5 – DOES THE FOOTPRINT PROVIDE A PRECISE ESTIMATE OF HUMAN IMPACT?

To secure wide public acceptance, footprints do not exaggerate the severity of the ecological situation. Rather, they offer an underestimate of the true human impact on the earth. Still, in spite of their systematic underestimates of the human impact on the planet, the ecological footprint calculations show that humanity uses more than the biosphere can regenerate. Also, in most footprint assessments, we use official data – and not because they are the most reliable. This is to illustrate that, once these official statistics are interpreted from an ecological perspective, significant new conclusions emerge. (See also Question 14 on the possibilities for including more impacts into future ecological footprint analyses.)

QUESTION 6 – IF NOT, DON'T WE NEED A MORE ACCURATE POLICY TOOL?

Greater accuracy is always desirable but, more often than not, the data are lacking. The authors challenge governments and other agencies to collect the data that would be required to support more detailed ecological footprint analyses. Yet the authors also realize the dangers of 'analysis paralysis' – there is no need to delay action by working out our impacts to the fifth decimal place if we already know that we have a problem.

– good Q.

QUESTION 7 – ECOLOGICAL FOOTPRINTING SEEMS TO BE VERY 'TWO DIMENSIONAL'. IT TALKS ABOUT LAND AREAS, BUT WHAT ABOUT HEIGHT AND DEPTH? COULDN'T OUR ECONOMY CONTINUE TO EXPAND BY BUILDING UPWARDS OR DOWNWARDS?

Areas are used as measurement units, since most life processes depend on surface area. This surface area is ultimately bounded by the size of the globe. There are life-supporting functions happening under the earth and in the atmosphere. If possible, the authors' assign them to the surface under or over which they occur (though we cannot yet account for many processes since no reliable data exist). To avoid counting areas twice, the footprint method only accounts for the dominant function. In other words, we only include uses of nature that mutually exclude each other on the same plot of the planet's surface. An example of how footprinting could be expanded to take into account 'shadow', overlapping land areas is given in the section on water. (See Box 5.8.)

In essence, the planet's limited surface serves as a proxy measure of the limited capacity of nature. It frames the core question for sustainability more precisely: How can people secure their quality of life within the two hectares, or so, of bioproductive space that exist for every individual on this planet?

QUESTION 8 – WHY HAVE THE FOOTPRINT NUMBERS GONE UP?

The footprint sizes reported here are in many cases larger than the ones given in *Our Ecological Footprint* (Wackernagel and Rees, 1996)[2] and in some other papers written by the authors. Rather than increased consumption, these figures have changed due to significant advances in the accounting methodology. Now we include sea space; consumption is documented more completely; and pasture and forest yields as well as CO_2 absorption are based on more realistic assessments.

QUESTION 9 – ECOLOGICAL FOOTPRINTING DEALS ONLY WITH MEASURING THE 'MEANS OF NATURE'. THIS SEEMS TO IGNORE FACTORS SUCH AS HUMAN HEALTH AND THE WELL-BEING OF SOCIETY. AREN'T THESE IMPORTANT?

The ecological footprint does not measure sustainability as a whole. It captures only ecological and distributional aspects of it. It does not inform about people's quality of life. Sustainability requires satisfying lives for all, within the means of nature. To measure to what extent people are satisfied with their lives, the think-tank Redefining Progress is now venturing a 'satisfaction barometer' that can complement the ecological footprint. Have a look at the section on linking ecological sustainability and social sustainability indicators in Chapter 2.

QUESTION 10 – ISN'T SUSTAINABILITY ABOUT THE TRIPLE BOTTOM-LINE: ENVIRONMENT, SOCIETY AND ECONOMY? YOU SEEM TO IGNORE THE ECONOMY.

Focusing on the tension between maintaining ecological integrity and securing satisfying lives is, the authors believe, more effective in capturing the sustainability dilemma than the often used three interlocking circles metaphor, for various reasons:

- Economy is not an end but a means. It is a means to secure quality of life and should be organized in a way so as not to exceed the means of nature. So yes, a healthy economy is important, but the authors do not believe that it should be treated as an end in itself.
- The underlying struggle is between people wanting to live well (an important and absolutely legitimate claim) and the need to live within the means of nature (a thermodynamic necessity in order to maintain themselves). The problem is that living well is currently secured through continually increasing supplies, but the ecological capacity to provide these supplies is limited. Also, without the integrity of the ecological capacity, the provision for human life is put at risk.
- Environment, society and economy are not three equal concepts. Functionally, the economy is part of society, which is part of the biosphere – in other words, rather than three interlocking circles, they should be portrayed as three concentric circles (see Figure 1.2).

Having three simultaneous aims is hard to communicate. Think of soccer: if three teams play against each other, it becomes confusing. Two teams make a far better soccer game (see Figure 6.1). It is more exciting and easier to follow. One team on the soccer field makes for no game at all. So having a clear tension between two competing goals, both of which we need to achieve, more accurately reflects the trade-offs we are facing. Even though the interlocking circles model sounds convincing and comprehensive in the beginning, it does not illuminate the underlying sustainability conflicts in the end. Nor does it help to explore the relationships between the different elements of sustainability. It diffuses the discussion and makes it unnecessarily complex. A lack of clarity tends to protect 'business as usual'.

QUESTION 11 – ISN'T THERE MORE TO SOCIAL NEEDS THAN MERELY 'QUALITY LIVES FOR ALL'?

'Quality lives for all' is a shorthand for good institutions, equity and fairness, safety and security, excitement and opportunities, material

Figure 6.1 *The real challenge is the play-off between the 'wants' of society (quality of life goals) and environmental limits. The economy should be viewed as no more than the playing field*

and mental well-being. It requires, no doubt, a healthy economy that makes sure we can live well on nature's interest and that supports people's aspirations for satisfying lives (but, by definition, this cannot be a conventional growth-based economy).

QUESTION 12 – WE ARE USING UP MANY OF OUR MATERIAL RESOURCES SUCH AS COPPER AND TIN. HOW DOES ECOLOGICAL FOOTPRINTING MEASURE THIS RESOURCE DEPLETION?

In the environmental debate of the 1970s, most attention was given to the non-renewable parts of the world's natural capital. The prime reason was the concern that the finite stocks of fossil fuel, minerals and ores, all essential ingredients of industrial processes, will eventually be exhausted. Only recently has it dawned on society that the renewable parts of natural capital, including its many life-support services, are even more critical and likely to be the first victims of an ecological collapse.

Resources such as copper and tin are accounted for through the mechanical impacts and energy use of extracting and processing the ores. In our current accounts, the energy requirements for the ores are included and more recently we have also included an estimate of the direct disruption caused by mining.

QUESTION 13 – WHY DO YOU GIVE SO MUCH ATTENTION TO THE RENEWABLE RESOURCES? AREN'T THEY SUSTAINABLE ALREADY?

It is the renewable natural capital that is a non-negotiable condition for life. In spite of their misleading name, renewable resources can be depleted if overused or misused. If we draw upon them more rapidly than they can regenerate, or exceed their capacity in some other way, they will be diminished. Renewable resources are only sustainable if we do not overuse them. Therefore, it is the biosphere's potential to renew itself that becomes the limiting factor for maintaining long-term human well-being.

QUESTION 14 – HOW DOES ECOLOGICAL FOOTPRINTING DEAL WITH POLLUTION SUCH AS SULPHUR DIOXIDE?

The ecological footprint only addresses human uses of nature that can potentially be sustainable. In other words, there is no ecological footprint for plutonium or other accumulating toxic materials. It is reasonable to say that these substances are fundamentally at odds with sustainability and must be phased out. Since the footprint does not (and cannot) include them, they need to be monitored separately. Renewable materials, on the other hand, do have a footprint. Some of these footprints are not included in current calculations due to lack of data. In theory it is possible to calculate the loss of bioproductivity from pollutants such as SO_2. A certain amount of acidity may be tolerated or absorbed by soils. More may lead to a loss of bioproductivity (which would add to the footprint). Too much SO_2 may start to accumulate and leave soils damaged. As the relationship between pollution and damage is subject to geographical differences and not always linear, generic assumptions about pollution and footprints are data-intensive and therefore difficult to make.

QUESTION 15 – WHAT HAS ECOLOGICAL FOOTPRINTING GOT TO DO WITH LOCAL AGENDA 21?

Many Local Agenda 21 initiatives have used the ecological footprint as a framework for their ecological thinking. It provides the context in which people's quality of life needs to be defined, and the ecological boundaries within which people's quality of life needs to be achieved. With more advanced footprint tools, the authors have been able to assist municipalities in developing more detailed accounts for their ecological impacts and demands.

QUESTION 16 – ECOLOGICAL FOOTPRINTING IMPLIES THAT TRADE IS BAD. HOW ARE HIGHLY POPULOUS COUNTRIES OR COMMUNITIES MEANT TO SURVIVE?

The ecological footprint does not condemn trade. It merely makes ecological trade imbalances visible. We believe that the world is more likely to be a sustainable place if every region lives within its own carrying capacity. This does not mean that it must live only on local products, but that the footprint of its imports should be similar to the footprint of its exports. If we can only consume up to the capacity of the region, there is much more direct and immediate feedback to the scale of our economy. Otherwise it becomes easy to put the cost on 'distant elsewheres'. Kirkpatrick Sale compared this view with the ice-making tray. Without the divisions in the tray, carrying water becomes hazardous – with the tray, the water is more stable. Similarly, if we have to live within our ecological capacity (and still can have ecologically balanced trade with other regions) the overall effect would be global stability.

QUESTION 17 – THE ECOLOGICAL FOOTPRINT DOES NOT APPEAR TO RECOGNIZE THAT AS TECHNOLOGY IMPROVES WE CAN COPE WITH MORE PEOPLE AND LESS LAND PER CAPITA. FOR EXAMPLE, WE HAVE ADAPTED OUR AGRICULTURAL SYSTEMS TO PRODUCE MORE FOOD PER HECTARE. WHY CAN'T THIS CONTINUE?

There is no assumption in the footprint about what technology can or cannot do. It accounts for the use of nature and compares it to the capacity of nature. And indeed, some technologies help to produce more per unit of land (in some cases, however, permanently damaging the soils or biodiversity). The more threatening issue that the ecological footprint tries to articulate is 'overshoot', which means that ecological capacity can be used beyond its regenerative capacity. While some technologies exist to reduce human impact, most technology has been used to gain access to limited resources at a faster rate and with more ease. In other words, whilst we have the technological capacity for a sustainable world, we seem to choose technologies that increase our overall footprint and increase human overshoot. The ecological footprint only monitors how successful we are in applying the technology that helps us live within the means of nature.

QUESTION 18 – A BIG PART OF ANY FOOTPRINT APPEARS TO BE DUE TO ENERGY USE. IF WE SWITCH TO ENERGY SOURCES, SUCH AS SOLAR ENERGY, THAT DO NOT ADD CARBON DIOXIDE TO THE ATMOSPHERE, WON'T THIS DRAMATICALLY REDUCE OUR FOOTPRINT TO THE POINT THAT THE CONCEPT IS MEANINGLESS?

True, in industrial countries, fossil fuel use accounts for about half of the footprint. In countries that rely more on traditional fuels, the percentage is much smaller. Still, the non-fossil footprint of some industrial countries remains larger than their own ecological capacity and their per capita consumption is higher than the average earthshare.

Moving to some non-fossil energy systems such as wind and solar energy (and the 'fifth fuel' of energy conservation) does have a great potential to reduce our footprints. However, the energy footprint will not become zero since it still requires space (and possibly also requires the use of fossil fuels in their production and installation). An extreme case is ethanol produced from biomass. Production may actually lead to a *larger* footprint per unit than the area necessary to absorb the CO_2 of the fossil fuel equivalent.

QUESTION 19 – WHAT ABOUT NUCLEAR POWER?

Nuclear power, the authors believe, has at least as large an ecological impact as fossil fuel if we consider the risk of long-term damage. Assessments of future risk are not, however, part of the current footprint methodology – apart from anything else the data are subject to much controversy. However, the losses through Chernobyl alone suggest a footprint per nuclear energy unit larger than that of fossil fuel. Life cycle studies of nuclear energy also reveal the fact that a substantial amount of pollution is produced in the production and processing of nuclear materials and the construction of power stations. That is why we normally assume the nuclear footprint as equal to the fossil fuel footprint (rather than assuming it to be zero). There is every danger of the fossil fuel or nuclear power debate turning into a paper cup versus plastic cup confrontation which avoids the real issue – they are both as bad as each other.

QUESTION 20 – WHAT CAN ECOLOGICAL FOOTPRINT ANALYSIS TELL US ABOUT THE FUTURE OF THE PLANET? ARE WE ALL DOOMED?

The footprint is not about how bad things are. It just makes our ecological reality visible. It helps us to react and avoid unnecessary destruction and suffering. In the past, new thinking about the world has helped humanity become more enlightened. Now too, we need different tools to react to new challenges. Ecological scarcity is a reality; it is not a product of the footprint calculation, but merely a conclusion. The footprint helps us to decide more wisely how to live in an age of scarcity. Footprint analysis also helps us see the good news. There are many examples in the world of people, groups and even societies who have been able to secure a high quality of life on impressively small footprints. They prove that it is possible to live well within nature's interest.

NOTES

1   To foster further debate and participation, the authors set up the ecofootprints email discussion group in early 1999. To join this group, send a blank email to ecofootprints-subscribe@egroups.com
2   http://www.newsociety.com/oef.html

Chapter 7

Global and National Footprints

'Though we dance to the beat of a different drum; we can learn to live together under the same sun' (Lyrics from the album 'People' released in 1995 to celebrate the fiftieth anniversary of the UN)

In 1999, Mathis Wackernagel and his team produced the second 'Footprint of Nations' report which analysed and compared national footprints.[1] This report examined 52 nations, including most of those discussed in the World Economic Forum's *Global Competitiveness Report* together with five others.[2] These nations account for 80 per cent of the world population and generate over 90 per cent of the World Domestic Product.

This assessment uses 1995 statistics from the UN, the most recent complete data set available in early 1999 when the study was completed. Using these sources the goal was to calculate national footprints and the ecological capacity for each country.[3] To put it more precisely, these calculations estimate the share of the global capacity that each nation occupies and the share that they contribute.

The compound footprinting methodology used is described in Chapter 4. In summary, each country is analysed on a spreadsheet with rows representing resources or product types. The columns specify the production, import and export of these resources or product types.

Box 7.1 Distribution of Footprints and Income Worldwide

How many people live on a footprint of less than the average American (9.6 ha) or more than the average Indian (1 ha)? How does this relate to real or comparative income distribution?

You can find the answers to these questions on the Internet at http://www.ecologicalfootprint.com.

Consumption is calculated by adding imports to production and subtracting exports. Using global average productivity data,[4] consumption is translated into land and water areas.

Energy consumption is also estimated using energy production figures adjusted for the embodied energy in imports and exports. This apparent consumption of energy is converted into a land area. For fossil fuel, this conversion is based on the forested area required to sequestrate the carbon emissions arising from the use of fossil fuels. As discussed elsewhere in this book, this is an underestimate of the true spatial impact of fossil fuel use.

The existing bioproductive area is reduced by a 'symbolic' 12 per cent for biodiversity preservation. The authors term the remaining 88 per cent the available biocapacity. The bioproductive areas that would be required to sustain a country (the demand) on the one hand, and available bioproductive areas on the other (the supply), are then summarized as shown in Table 7.1. To make the results comparable among different nations, the areas are converted into bioproductive space with world average productivity. Comparing adjusted areas rather than the direct physical extensions is more meaningful since land can vary greatly in terms of its quality.[5] By adjusting land for its bioproductivity, the comparisons show more directly the different use and supply of overall ecological capacity. Using land corrected for world average productivity also allows for a more meaningful comparison of national data.

LEAGUE OF NATIONS

Table 7.2 summarizes the results of the latest 'Footprints of Nations' study of average per capita footprint for each country along with the amount of bioproductive land available within that nation's borders.

If the footprint exceeds the available biologically productive area of the country, it runs an ecological deficit. In this case, the country's area alone cannot provide sufficient ecological services to satisfy its population's current patterns of consumption. Consequently, it needs to import its missing ecological capacity – or deplete its natural capital stocks.

For example, the Netherlands is listed as having available within its boundaries ecological capacity equivalent to 1.5 ha per capita of world average bioproductive space (including sea). This is around four times more than the actual land area available per person – a reflection of the high productivity of the soils. Despite this, the actual consumption of the average Dutch citizen still exceeds the locally available ecological capacity by a factor of three, with a requirement of 5.6 ha per capita.

A few countries – New Zealand is the most notable example – have more ecological capacity available than their footprints occupy. This is indicated by positive numbers in the ecological deficit column, and rather than deficits, they have ecological remainders (the grey line

doesn't flow very well – the whole book.

Table 7.1 *The Canadians' Demand for and Supply of Carrying Capacity (1995)*

Demand Ecological footprint (per Canadian)	Total (ha/cap)	Equivalence factor	Equivalent total (ha/per cap)
Fossil energy	3.0	1.2	3.5
Built-up area	0.2	2.8	0.7
Arable land	0.5	2.8	1.3
Pasture	1.6	0.4	0.7
Forest	0.9	1.2	1.0
Sea	1.1	0.1	0.1
Total used			**7.2**

Supply Biocapacity of Canada and the world (per person)	Yield factor	Physical extension Canada (ha/cap)	Yield adjusted equivalent area	
			Canada (ha/per cap)	World (ha/per cap)
CO$_2$ absorp land	0.00	0.0	0.00	
Built-up area	1.06	0.23	0.7	0.17
Arable land	1.06	1.55	4.7	0.75
Pasture	1.05	1.04	0.5	0.19
Forest	0.44	15.33	8.0	1.05
Sea	1.00	3.29	0.7	0.03
Total existing		**21.4**	**14.0**	**2.2**
Total available (minus 12% for biodiversity protection)			**12.3**	**1.9**

Note: This table compares the ecological footprint of the Canadians to the ecological capacity available in Canada and the world. Note that the results of the footprint as well as of the yield equivalent areas are expressed in units of average space with world average productivity. For example, to get the yield adjusted area expressed in these units, the true physical extension is multiplied by the yield factors (the productivity of Canadian arable land compared to world average arable land) and by the equivalence factors (the productivity of global average arable land as compared to global average space). Numbers do not add up due to rounding.

extends to the right of the centre line of Figure 7.2). While this reveals that the country is endowed with some 'spare' capacity, this capacity is seldom left unused or protected for biodiversity. More often it is used for the production of export goods.

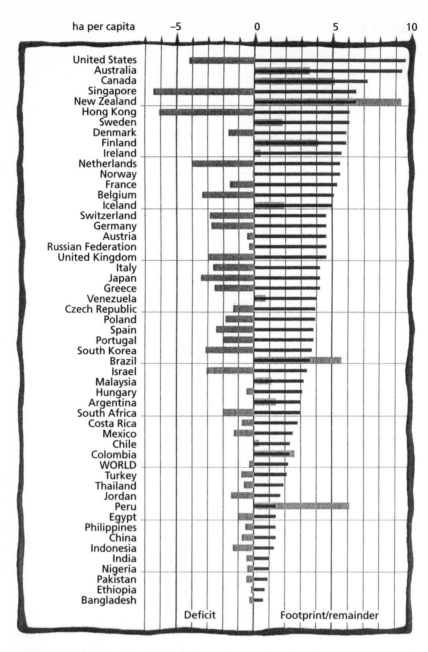

Note: The black line indicates the average per capita ecological footprint, the grey line indicates the extent to which the country could meet its needs from within its own bioproductive capacity – which includes land and sea. If the grey line extends to the right it indicates a national ecological remainder. If the grey line extends to the left it indicates a national ecological deficit

Figure 7.2 *Ranking of each nation by per capita footprint*

The national footprints can also be compared to what has previously been referred to as the average earthshare. A figure of 1.9 ha per capita was derived in Chapter 4. In the case of the US it can be seen that the average per capita footprint of 9.6 ha is close to five times the sustainable earthshare. Eleven of the 52 nations studied have a per capita footprint below the average earthshare. Amongst these are the two most populous countries of the world, China and India. These two alone account for more than one-third of the global population.

At 1995 consumption, population and technology levels, the 'Footprints of Nations' study showed that the 52 countries were exceeding their available biocapacity by 37 per cent – a clear case of overshoot. By including estimates for the consumption and capacity of the nations not included in the study – which together account for 20 per cent of the world population – it is suggested that globally the overshoot was 15 per cent. If we assume a constant per capita footprint up to 2000, the overshoot will have grown to 22 per cent. Obviously, if the 12 per cent of space put aside for preserving biodiversity should prove to be insufficient (as many conservation ecologists suggest), the global ecological deficit would be more dramatic.

ECOLOGICAL CAPACITY AND COMPETITIVENESS

In 2000, one of the largest private banks in the world, the Union Bancaire Privée (UBP), sponsored a study on the impact of ecological performance on competitiveness. Forty-four countries were investigated using ecological footprint analysis to indicate environmental sustainability. As they acknowledge in the introduction to the published report, UBP are well aware of the link between ecological performance and competitiveness:[6]

> *The transition to sustainability is necessary and, in the long term, inevitable. In a world of shrinking resources, those who first recognise the need for sustainability and adopt appropriate strategies will succeed best in future global competition. Directing investment towards sustainability will not only accelerate that transition, but also advance the combined interests of investors, governments, and the public at large.*

Taking as its starting point the national demand and supply assessments described earlier in this chapter, the study goes on to explore the relationship between footprints and economic performance, adopting the annual competitiveness index developed by the World Economic Forum (WEF) as the measure of global competitiveness.[7]

The report uses the terms developed in the financial markets: 'bulls' for the more competitive countries and 'bears' for those less competitive; it adds additional descriptors of 'red' or 'green' to indicate whether

Table 7.2 *The Ecological Footprints of Nations*

Nation	Population (1995)	Nation's average ecological footprint (ha per cap)	Nation's available biocapacity (ha per cap)
Argentina	34,768,000	3.0	4.4
Australia	17,862,000	9.4	12.9
Austria	8,045,000	4.6	4.1
Bangladesh	118,229,000	0.6	0.2
Belgium	10,535,000	5.1	1.7
Brazil	159,015,000	3.6	9.1
Canada	29,402,000	7.2	12.3
Chile	14,210,000	2.3	2.6
China	1,220,224,000	1.4	0.6
Colombia	35,814,000	2.3	4.9
Costa Rica	3,424,000	2.8	2.0
Czech Republic	10,263,000	3.9	2.6
Denmark	5,223,000	5.9	4.2
Egypt	62,096,000	1.4	0.5
Ethiopia	56,404,000	0.7	0.5
Finland	5,107,000	5.8	9.9
France	58,104,000	5.3	3.7
Germany	81,594,000	4.6	1.9
Greece	10,454,000	4.2	1.6
Hong Kong	6,123,000	6.1	0.0
Hungary	10,454,000	3.1	2.6
Iceland	269,000	5.0	6.8
India	929,005,000	1.0	0.5
Indonesia	197,460,000	1.3	2.6
Ireland	3,546,000	5.6	6.0
Israel	5,525,000	3.5	0.3
Italy	57,204,000	4.2	1.5
Japan	125,068,000	4.2	0.7
Jordan	4,215,000	1.6	0.2
Korea, Rep	44,909,000	3.7	0.4
Malaysia	20,140,000	3.2	4.3
Mexico	91,145,000	2.5	1.3
Netherlands	15,482,000	5.6	1.5
New Zealand	3,561,000	6.5	15.9
Nigeria	111,721,000	1.0	0.6
Norway	4,332,000	5.5	5.4
Pakistan	136,257,000	0.9	0.4
Peru	23,532,000	1.4	7.5
Philippines	67,839,000	1.4	0.8
Poland, Rep	38,557,000	3.9	2.0
Portugal	9,815,000	3.8	1.8
Russian Federation	148,460,000	4.6	4.3
Singapore	3,327,000	6.6	0.0
South Africa	41,465,000	3.0	1.0
Spain	39,627,000	3.8	1.4
Sweden	8,788,000	6.1	7.9
Switzerland	7,166,000	4.6	1.8
Thailand	58,242,000	1.9	1.3
Turkey	60,838,000	2.1	1.2
United Kingdom	58,301,000	4.6	1.5
United States	267,115,000	9.6	5.5
Venezuela	21,844,000	4.0	4.7
World	5,687,114,000	2.2	1.9

Note: For 52 countries, representing 80 per cent of the world population, this table lists its 1995 population, and its ecological footprint, available biocapacity and national ecological deficit for 1995 – three on a per capita basis and the last two in national

Nation's ecological deficit (if negative) (ha per cap)	Total eco-footprint of nation (km²)	Total available biocapacity of nation (km²)
1.4	1,060,000	1,542,000
3.5	1,672,000	2,305,000
−0.5	373,000	332,000
−0.3	659,000	275,000
−3.4	535,000	174,000
5.6	5,670,000	14,545,000
5.1	2,122,000	3,615,000
0.3	329,000	372,000
−0.8	17,311,000	7,323,000
2.6	828,000	1,765,000
−0.8	96,000	68,000
−1.4	405,000	263,000
−1.7	309,000	221,000
−1.0	896,000	294,000
−0.2	389,000	274,000
4.1	298,000	506,000
−1.6	3,062,000	2,153,000
−2.8	3,788,000	1,540,000
−2.6	438,000	165,000
−6.1	375,000	2,400
−0.5	322,000	269,000
1.9	13,000	18,000
−0.5	9,353,000	4,472,000
1.4	2,509,000	5,199,000
0.4	197,000	213,000
−3.1	191,000	17,000
−2.8	2,414,000	837,000
−3.5	5,252,000	873,000
−1.4	69,000	8,200
−3.2	1,649,000	199,000
1.1	642,000	872,000
−1.3	2,306,000	1,158,000
−4.1	867,000	238,000
9.4	230,000	565,000
−0.4	1,069,000	656,000
−0.1	237,000	234,000
−0.5	1,278,000	552,000
6.1	341,000	1,766,000
−0.7	965,000	523,000
−1.9	1,511,000	786,000
−2.0	368,000	172,000
−0.4	6,839,000	6,314,000
−6.5	219,000	1,000
−1.9	1,224,000	415,000
−2.5	1,524,000	553,000
1.8	534,000	695,000
−2.9	333,000	127,000
−0.7	1,120,000	740,000
−0.8	1,260,000	756,000
−3.0	2,667,000	903,000
−4.1	25,532,000	14,697,000
0.7	869,000	1,018,000
−0.3	126,080,000	110,091,000

absolutes. The results are calculated for 1995, and all areas are expressed in bioproductive area with world-average yields. This means that areas with higher productivity appear proportionally larger in these accounts. (Tables and calculations adapted from Wackernagel et al (1999).

the nation is in ecological debt or credit. Thus, each country can be assigned to one of four categories. The following descriptions are reproduced from the published study:

- *Green bulls* – Nations attaining a high degree of competitiveness while operating within their ecological capacity; these are ecological creditors who are also economically successful.
- *Red bulls* – Nations attaining an equally high degree of competitiveness, but which operate beyond their ecological limits; these are economic successes but ecological debtors.
- *Green bears* – Nations with a low competitiveness ranking but an ecological surplus; these are struggling economically but are ecological creditors.
- *Red bears* – Nations with a low competitiveness ranking and ecological debt; these are both struggling economically and accumulating ecological debt.

The ecological capacity and competitiveness of the 44 nations studied is illustrated in Figure 7.3. There are few green bears – that is, non-competitive countries in ecological credit. According to the report's authors, these are 'without exception ... suffering or recovering from violent internal conflicts'. Red bulls – competitive countries in ecological debt – are the most numerous. This apparent contradiction between ecological and economic well-being can easily be explained. The countries in this category tend to be those with a long history of accumulating financial capital dating back to a period when ecological resources were not as scarce. In effect, they had a 'head start' at a time of abundant resources. Presently, they are therefore in the privileged position of being able to afford to import, or appropriate in some other way, ecological capacity from outside of their own borders. In many cases they may also be depleting their own natural capital. This situation is tenuous. If these countries were to become less competitive they would be unable to purchase the resources that they need. They would soon become red bears.

Undoubtedly, it is the red bears – those that have an ecological debt and are non-competitive – that will experience the greatest difficulty adjusting their economies to meet future ecological challenges. They are amongst the economically weakest countries yet currently rely on purchasing ecological capacity from elsewhere, or depleting their own natural capital. They are unlikely to be able to wield sufficient economic muscle to secure the goods and services that they require. To avoid internal conflict, upheavals and scarcity they must act to improve the efficiency with which they use resources.

The green bulls would seem to be in the best position. They are competitive nations in ecological credit. However, if they tread the same economic path as the other industrialized nations, they will also

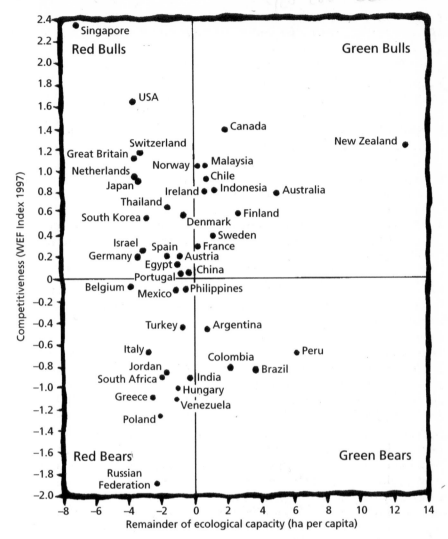

Figure 7.3 *Ecological capacity and competitiveness*

end up in ecological debt. Without a change in economic strategy they will lose their competitive ecological advantage.

The report's authors conclude that 'the current loose connection between ecological capacity may well become tighter'. Eco-efficiency is set to become an important determinant of competitiveness in the global economy.

The UBP study, along with the rest of this chapter, deals extensively with quantitative assessments of ecological demand and supply. This tends to exclude many audiences – in particular those who are looking for a more immediate message, one that can communicate the complex matters of ecological capacity in an entertaining, informative or

great examples to back up blabbling

Box 7.2 Barbados – Horrors and Hopes

The first UN global conference after the Rio UNCED meeting was held in Barbados. A parallel activity offered an opportunity to citizens to exhibit their concerns about sustainability by clear declarations of the problems ('horrors') and role models or best practice solutions ('hopes') – it was called the 'Village of Hope'. Three thousand Barbadians put it together and over 45,000 people paid to visit the village (20 per cent of the population).

Out of it has come a permanent Future Centre developed in the house and grounds of an old plantation house. Already the Centre is working with five government ministries, major supermarkets, hardware stores, property management companies, energy and water suppliers and banks. A powerful tool used to engage the thousands of visitors is a presentation combining 'footprints' and the Swedish 'Natural Step'.

The footprint deficit for Barbados appears to be 2.8 ha per capita and ratio of demand to supply is nine! And yet in the 1940s and 1950s it was less than one. At that time Barbados was largely self-sufficient. This represents a nine-fold increase in resource use in 50 years.

Source: Contributed by Dr Colin Hudson and Maureen Watson, The Future Centre, Edgehill, St. Thomas, Barbados

---

resonant manner. It is worth pointing out, therefore, that many programmes aimed at engaging the public have used the ecological footprint concept to successfully convey aspects of sustainability. One permanent exhibition of note is in the Future Centre in Barbados (see Box 7.2).

THE CHINA SYNDROME

> *'No country better typifies the confluence of trends set out in this report – nor the challenges they pose to environmental quality and public health – than does modern China'* (World Resources 1998–99: A Guide to the Global Environment[9])

Amongst those countries with a low per capita footprint are the two most populous in the world; China and India (see Table 7.3). Together they account for more than one-third of the global population. Both are members of the exclusive one billion club – China has a population of more than 1.2 billion and India's numbers passed the billion mark in the autumn of 1999. Together the 11 countries with the lowest per capita footprint – those below the average earthshare – account for more than half of the global population.

Concern over the development path being taken by China – the so-called China Factor – remains a common thread running through many discussions of world resource scarcity. If China were to increase

Box 7.3 The New Economics Foundation's Green League

In 1993, the New Economics Foundation was invited by *The Independent* newspaper to compile a league table comparing the environmental performance of the world's developed countries. The Foundation considered 11 key environmental indicators using mostly 1990 and 1991 data from the OECD.[8] Although this study uses data four or five years older than the 'Footprint of Nations' report presented here, there is significant agreement between the Green League assessment (the higher the number of points the better the environmental performance) and the ecological footprint score.

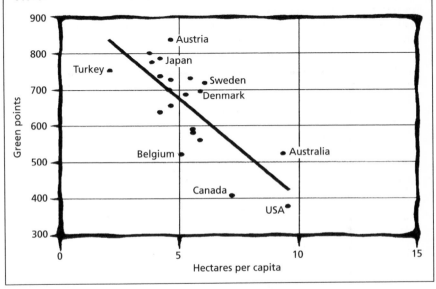

its per capita consumption to that of – for example – the US whilst other countries continued along their growth paths, could the global environment cope? While from an ethical perspective the affluent countries have no business condemning China for extending its footprints, ecologically speaking, there is not enough planet for this 'business as usual' approach. This shows the fundamental conflicts we are facing as we move towards sustainability. The Worldwatch Institute points out:

> 'China is teaching us that the Western industrial model is not viable, simply because there are not enough resources. Global land and water resources are not sufficient to satisfy the growing grain needs in China if it continues along the current development path... If carbon emissions per person in China ever reach the current US level, this alone would roughly double global emissions.'[10]

Box 7.4 Purchasing Power and Footprint

The graph below illustrates the close relationship between the traditional economic measure of average GDP – the total output of goods and services here adjusted for purchasing power parity with the US dollar – and the average per capita ecological footprint for the 52 nations covered by the study. All data are for the year 1995.

Although it is difficult to draw firm conclusions without an in-depth analysis, it would appear that the largely linear relationship between purchasing power and footprint breaks down at high levels of wealth. Switzerland, for example, has a footprint quite low relative to its financial status. Australia, on the other hand, has a high footprint relative to its purchasing power. There are also a significant number of countries – the Russian Federation being the most notable – where the footprint is higher than what one would expect based on spending power alone.

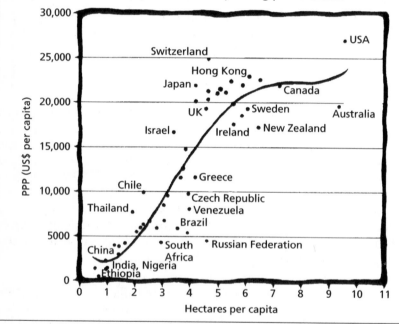

What started out as the 'China Factor' has turned into more of a syndrome. The population of India is expected to overtake that of China by 2050, representing a general trend of increasing numbers from the poorer countries. All of the other 11 'low footprint' countries are also predicted to experience significant population growth in the period to 2050.

Simple ecological footprint calculations can shed some useful light on this debate. The footprint of the average American, just for food, fibres, timber, and absorbing the CO_2 released by fossil fuel consumption, adds up to about 9.6 ha of bioproductive space. If we generously assume that the area of bioproductive space (including land and sea)

Table 7.3 *Breakdown of Footprint by Land Type for China, India and the US (ha per capita), 1995 data*

Land type	China	India	USA
Fossil energy	0.6	0.2	5.8
Built-up area	0.0	0.0	0.7
Arable land	0.6	0.6	1.0
Pasture	0.1	0.1	0.9
Forest	0.1	0.1	1.1
Sea	0.0	0.0	0.1
Total	**1.4**	**1.0**	**9.6**

Note: Adjusted to world average bioproductive area

remains at 12.5 billion ha and a meagre 12 per cent of this area is set aside for other species, then the approximate number of people that the planet could sustain at US levels of consumption can be determined as follows:

12.5 billion ha/9.6 ha per person x 88 per cent = 1.2 billion people

Interestingly, this is close to the lower estimates of carrying capacity written about by notable sustainability researchers such as Anne and Paul Ehrlich[11] and Marcia and David Pimentel.[12] Of course, the simple calculation presented makes no assumptions about improvements in technology or the potential benefits that would accrue from efficiency savings. It just assumes extending current practice to all people.

A more optimistic scenario which saw the world population maintain a good quality of life with a footprint of 1.4 ha – the current level of the average Chinese footprint – would permit a sustainable global population of nearly eight billion:

12.5 billion ha/1.4 ha per person x 88 per cent = 7.9 billion people

Such a transformation of our relationship with the natural world is – the authors believe – entirely possible. To make this happen would require a significant rethink of our institutional structures, changes in the way taxes are applied, encouragement of eco-efficient technologies, and a massive redesign of our urban infrastructure.

The outlook is promising. Numerous case studies of 'Factor 4' resource savings, and beyond, appear in the work of Amory and Hunter Lovins from the Rocky Mountain Institute.[13] Meanwhile, individuals such as Simon Fairlie, Vicki Robin and Joe Dominguez, and organizations such as the Centre for a New American Dream have also proven inspirational in their commitment to demonstrating the joys of living better on less.[14]

As elsewhere, the ecological footprint offers no prognosis, only a straightforward diagnosis. For a world sick with China syndrome, and a severe case of 'affluenza', the authors' advice would be to seek help.

NOTES

1   The original study of national footprints was: Mathis Wackernagel, Larry Onisto, Alejandro Callejas Linares, Ina Susana López Falfán, Jesus Méndez García, Ana Isabel Suárez Geurrero, Ma Guadalupe Suárez Geurrero, 1997, *Ecological Footprints of Nations: How Much Nature Do They Use? How Much Nature Do They Have?* Commissioned by the Earth Council for the Rio+5 Forum; it is distributed by the International Council for Local Environmental Initiatives, Toronto. The calculation method is also described in Mathis Wackernagel, Larry Onisto, Patricia Bello, Alejandro Callejas Linares, Ina Susana López Falfán, Jesus Méndez García, Ana Isabel Suárez Geurrero and Ma Guadalupe Suárez Geurrero, 1999, 'National Natural Capital Accounting with the Ecological Footprint Concept', *Ecological Economics*, Vol 29, No 3, June 1999. The update for 1995, commissioned by the Union Bancaire Privée of Geneva was completed in July 1999. The update for 1996, in collaboration with the Union Bancaire Privée and WWF International, will be completed in 2000 and will include 150 countries. The full spreadsheets for this study are available on the internet from Redefining Progress, http://www. rprogress.org. Linked from http://www.ecologicalfootprint.com

2   Two countries of the World Economic Forum's *Global Competitiveness Report* are missing in this analysis: Luxembourg and Taiwan, as they do not appear in UN statistics

3   All the main sources used in this report stem from United Nations documents. The data sources are (1): United Nations, 1997, *1995 International Trade Statistics Yearbook*, vol 1, New York: Department for Economic and Social Information and Policy Analysis, Statistical Division (2): United Nations Conference on Trade and Development (UNCTAD), 1996, *UNCTAD Commodity Yearbook 1996*, New York and Geneva: United Nations (3): Food and Agriculture Organisation of the United Nations (FAO), 1997, *FAO Yearbook: Production 1996*, vol 50, Rome: FAO (4): Food and Agriculture Organisation of the United Nations (FAO), 1996, *FAO Yearbook: Trade 1995*, vol 49, Rome: FAO (5): Food and Agriculture Organisation of the United Nations (FAO), 1997, *FAO Yearbook: Forest Production 1995*, Rome: FAO (WRI): World Resources Institute, 1998, *World Resources 1998–1999*, Washington, DC: World Resources Institute, UNEP, UNDP, The World Bank Food and Agriculture Organisation of the United Nations (FAO), 1997, *State of the World's Forests*, Rome: FAO

4   Most world average productivities are taken from: Food and Agriculture Organisation of the United Nations (FAO), 1997, *FAO Yearbook: Production 1996*, vol 50, Rome: FAO. These data can also be accessed from the on-line database of FAO http://apps.fao.org/ last accessed on 26 November, 1999

5   Obviously, footprint studies could also be expressed in the direct land areas occupied. An excellent study of The Netherlands, undertaken by the RIVM, compares the world average approach to the one using land areas directly. For The Netherlands, the direct approach reduces their productivity adjusted footprint of 5.6 hectares per capita to 2.4 hectares per capita since The Netherlands has highly productive soils and is importing produce from highly productive regions of the globe. The flip side of this, of course, is that this makes the footprints of those having to use lower quality land look bigger – an equity issue not captured when actual yields are the only benchmark. It also answers another question: not how many earths it would take to support all the people's footprints, but how many Hollands it would take. Since humanity has to live within global capacity (rather than Dutch capacity), the authors feel that the first question is the more relevant one – and to answer it we need to adjust the productivity of the various ecological spaces. For more details, see Detlef van Vuuren, Smeets and de Kruijf; 'The Ecological Footprint of Benin, Bhutan, Costa Rica and The Netherlands' RIVM Report 807005004, July, 1999. Available from RIVM, PO Box 1, 3720 BA Bilthoven, The Netherlands. This report provides arguably the most advanced critique of the ecological footprint methodology.

6   Sturm, A, Wackernagel, M, Müller, K, 2000, *The Winners and Losers in Global Competition: Why Eco-efficiency Reinforces Competitiveness: A Study of 44 Nations*, Zürich: Verlag Rüegger

7   World Economic Forum (WEF), 1997, *Global Competitiveness Report 1997*, Geneva: WEF: http://www.weforum.org

8   'A Green League of Nations: Relative Environmental Performance in OECD Countries', 1993, New Economics Foundation, London

9   *World Resources 1998–99*, published by Oxford University Press, 1998. A joint publication by The World Resources Institute, The United Nations Environment Programme, The United Nations Development Programme and The World Bank

10 *State of the World 1998*, 'The future of growth', p13. Published by Earthscan, London, 1998

11 Many studies agree, as David Willey also confirms in his survey essay called 'optimum population', that if people should have the opportunity to live at the material level of average Western European residents, the biosphere may only be able to sustain 2 billion people. Surprisingly, the various studies by David and Marcia Pimentel and their team; the Hunger Project (by R W Kates, R S Chen, T E Downing and their collaborators); Anne and Paul Ehrlich, Gretchen Daily; Sandra Postel; Mathis Wackernagel, William Rees and their collaborators; or John Holdren, reproduce this result within small margins of differences once these studies are adjusted to make them comparable. The most significant adjustment is aligning the studies' assumption about the population's average standard of living. With this adjustment alone, the carrying capacity numbers for the biosphere fall within the range of 1 to 3 billion people. Willey, David, 1999, Optimum World Population, draft report to the Optimum Population Trust, unpublished, Llanfallteg, Dyfed SA34 OUW, UK. This recognition goes back over 30 years, including an earlier study by Paul Ehrlich, 1971, 'The population crisis: Where we stand', in *Population, Environment and People*, ed, Noël Hinrichs, New York: McGraw-Hill, pp8–16

12   Pimentel, D, 1994, 'Natural resources and an optimum human popula-
      tion', *Earth Island Journal*, Summer 1994, vol 9, issue 3. Available on the
      internet: http://www.econet.apc.org/ei/journal/naturres.html, last
      accessed 22/1/99. Or see D Pimentel, O Bailey, P Kim, E Mullaney,
      J Calabrese, L Walman, F Nelson and X Yao, 1999, 'Will Limits of the
      Earth's Resources Control Human Numbers?' *Environment, Development,
      and Sustainability*, vol 1, 1999, pp19–39
13   *Factor Four: Doubling Wealth, Halving Resource Use*, 1998, Ernst von
      Weizsäcker, Amory B Lovins, L Hunter Lovins; *Natural Capitalism: The
      Next Industrial Revolution*, 1999, Paul Hawken, Amory B Lovins, L Hunter
      Lovins; both by Earthscan Publications, London
14   Visit their website at www.newdream.org (last accessed on 24 November
      1999)

looks @ the regional + national prob. + worldwide prob.

Regional Footprinting

'The view from our backyards is changing – and not always for the better. New roads and housing cut swaths through the landscape; the countryside seems half choked with pesticides and fertilisers, or ripped up for waste dumps and open cast mines' (Martin Wright, journalist, 1991)

TIDYING UP THE BACKYARD

What is the size of the 'backyard' needed to support a community, city or larger region?

The answer to this question can be helpful in a number of ways; to assist in planning decisions, as part of sustainable communities programmes, or to inform land use decisions.

The ecological impact of densely populated cities inevitably spreads well beyond their administrative boundaries. Hence some argue that the term 'sustainable city' is an oxymoron.[1] This is not necessarily the pattern everywhere. Until recently, the planned agriculture of China required that cities were surrounded by belts of agricultural land where food was produced for them. Such connection to the land is beginning to return in a very modest fashion through the rise in popularity of community farms and markets to serve urban districts.[2]

How far, and how much, the tentacles of large or small conurbations reach beyond a region can be revealed with a footprint analysis.

Those attempting to calculate the ecological footprint for a region, be it a town or larger administrative territory, will almost certainly face difficulties obtaining accurate data. Unlike buildings, households, and countries, the boundaries of regions are invariably poorly defined. Where there are no border controls, consumption data are rarely collected or even officially estimated.

Problems also arise when large (and unknown) numbers of people regularly move in and out of the region under study. The question then arises as to how the consumption of such individuals is to be apportioned. Similarly, if a region has a significant amount of resource-intensive industry, the products of which may well be consumed elsewhere, how should this be reflected in a regional footprint?

All these are questions which must be addressed before any regional analyses are undertaken.

If one has the time and resources to conduct primary research (surveys or other data sampling), or if one is fortunate enough to be studying a region where data are readily available, then most problems can be resolved or, at least, informed assumptions made.

This section describes some applications of footprinting at a regional level – from a city to an island.

THE SUSTAINABLE CITY?

As one of the globe's mega-cities, the metabolism of London has come under the close scrutiny of several groups.[3] In 1994, for example, Herbert Girardet showed how the footprint of London was close to that of the total productive land area of England.

Girardet views cities rather like giant consuming machines which metabolize large quantities of resources and spew out solid and gaseous wastes. To illustrate this model Girardet considered only a selection of key resources and pollutants (built land, wood products, food land and CO_2 emissions). He collected data on these and arrived at an estimated ecological footprint for London of 48,900,000 acres (about 20,000,000 ha).

The authors' updated analysis of London's footprint, with the benefit of more recent information and conversion factors, results in a figure lower than that calculated by Girardet (see Table 8.1). Not least, this is due to reductions in carbon emissions arising from the UK's recent 'dash for gas' in the electricity generation market.

When a fuller set of resources is taken into account, the footprint increases substantially. A rough estimate of the footprint of London, based on the UK per capita figure in the 'Footprint of Nations' study (see Chapter 7), shows a likely footprint in excess of 32 million ha (4.6 ha x 7,007,000 persons).

Girardet's approach of considering a selection of key indicators upon which to estimate the footprint of a conurbation is a sensible compromise where comprehensive data are unavailable or where one's interests are focused on a particular aspect of environmental impact.

London is far from being the only city to have had its backyard explored. Folke and his colleagues estimated the ecological footprint of the 29 largest cities of Baltic Europe, extrapolating from national average data and looking, similarly, at just a selection of resource inputs and waste outputs[5] – the consumption of food and wood and the assimilation of phosphorous, nitrogen and carbon.[6]

Table 8.1 *Updated Footprint of London*

	Annual consumption	Footprint conversion	Ha
Area – ha[a]	157,800	2.27	357,670
Carbon – t[b]	13,574,000	0.82	11,163,160
Wood products – t[c]	2,242,240	0.97	2,176,970
Food – all in t [d]			
Meat and meat products	324,284	0.53	172,600
Liquid and processed milk and cream	732,372	0.10	70,880
Seafood	58,298	4.49	262,000
Vegetables and vegetable products	728,728	0.23	167,870
Fresh and other fruit	440,880	0.46	201,200
Bread	233,193	1.73	402,650
		Total (rounded)	15,000,000

Note: Conversion factors used are already adjusted for equivalence and in places vary slightly from those given in Chapter 5 due to local adjustments or historical data variations.
a   Based on World Resource Data (1998–99). It is estimated that 80 per cent of Greater London is either built or degraded land.
b   Data from London Energy Study (1993)
c   Estimated per capita from national consumption data: 'Tomorrow's World' and 'Indicators of Sustainable Development'
d   Data on Greater London from Regional Trends 32 (1997)

As the land and water area required for waste assimilation was included, the footprints were large; at least 500 ha per hectare of city or in the range of 6–11.5 ha per person.[7] About two-thirds of this is accounted for by the space required to assimilate wastes.

URBAN ESTIMATES

Where specific data about a city are not known then its footprint can be estimated by apportioning the per capita impact as calculated in the 'Footprint of Nations' report. This is a similar approach to that taken by Folke and his colleagues as outlined earlier. In 1998 the authors illustrated the scale of impact of major cities in the UK in this manner. A circle representing the potential area of impact is shown drawn around selected cities (see Figure 8.2).

Of course, such an analysis provides only an initial guide to the size of the ecological hinterland of a particular urban area, taking no

*and given an [?] task
close to particular
at city's eco [?]
city's [?]*

Box 8.1 The Hague – Green City by the Sea[4]

In 1998 Hague City Council undertook an ecological footprint analysis of the city, presenting the results as part of a public sustainability indicators initiative. The Hague covers an area of more than 7000 ha. The ecological footprint of its residents is many times larger – more than two million hectares (4.9 ha per person) being needed to survive. The ecological footprint is presented as part of the Hague environmental thermometer monitoring system, which provides an insight into the quality and development of the local urban environment.

---

account of local variations. The obvious next stage is to try and gather more accurate consumption data for the area in question.

Several studies are presented, as much to illustrate the problems with data collection at this scale as to provide an accurate footprint figure.

OXFORDSHIRE'S SUSTAINABILITY GAP

In 1996 two of the authors (Simmons and Chambers) set out to explore the footprint of Oxfordshire in England using a prototype version of 'Stepwise', a computer-based programme aimed at simplifying the activity-based calculations of ecological footprints.[8]

For those not familiar with Oxfordshire, it is a relatively small, wealthy and fairly densely populated county in the south of England. The city of Oxford houses around one-fifth of the county's population.

Officers from the county planning department were able to provide some of the necessary data to calculate the county's footprint. Where local data were not available, they were estimated from regional or national sources.[9] Table 8.2 shows the data and conversions to footprint values.

With 0.5 ha of land per capita, Oxfordshire compares favourably with the average British figure of 0.35 ha.[10]

Using 'StepWise', a per capita footprint of 7.5 ha was calculated (see Table 8.2). Thus about fifteen times the land area of Oxfordshire is required just to support the consumption patterns of the inhabitants and local industry (assuming global average bioproductive space).

Although not able to capture all resource use, 'StepWise' proved useful in identifying the most significant areas of consumption to help target campaigns and support awareness-raising exercises aimed at moving towards more sustainable consumption patterns.

Collecting further data about local land productivities would allow us to compare Oxfordshire's supply with its demand. This is more easily determined by a compound footprinting approach, as the next example from Santiago, in Chile, illustrates.

United Kingdom

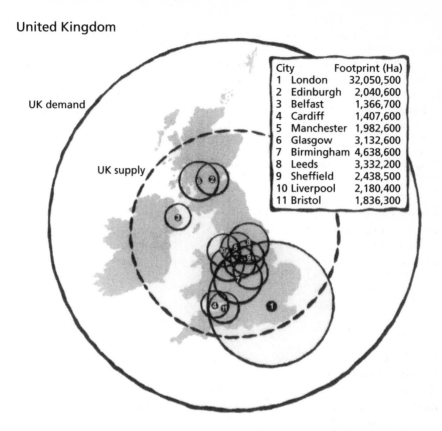

City		Footprint (Ha)
1	London	32,050,500
2	Edinburgh	2,040,600
3	Belfast	1,366,700
4	Cardiff	1,407,600
5	Manchester	1,982,600
6	Glasgow	3,132,600
7	Birmingham	4,638,600
8	Leeds	3,332,200
9	Sheffield	2,438,500
10	Liverpool	2,180,400
11	Bristol	1,836,300

Note: Based solely on national per capita consumption data. The outer solid circle represents the total UK ecological footprint expressed as world average productive space (the demand). The inner dashed circle shows the yield-adjusted biocapacity (the supply)

Figure 8.2 *Footprint of a selection of UK cities*

SUSTAINABLE SANTIAGO

As part of the Sustainable Santiago project, one of the authors (Wackernagel) was commissioned to estimate the ecological footprint of Santiago de Chile.[11]

The Santiago metropolitan area houses about 4.7 million people, 35.6 per cent of Chile's population. Other data were supplied by the local authorities and the International Council for Local Environmental Initiatives (ICLEI Latin America).

The city calculations were based on a previously calculated national footprint using 1993 data. The summary table – the footprint for an average citizen of Santiago – is shown in Table 8.3. Once the calculation for an average Chilean citizen was derived from national data, various adjustments were made to approximate variations in consump-

Table 8.2 *A Footprint Analysis of Oxfordshire*

Annual demand	Consumption (units)	Conversion (ha-years per unit)	Footprint (ha)
Electricity (GWh) – domestic	1042	111	115,287
Gas (GWh) – domestic	3760	41	155,847
Electricity – other (GWh)	2070	111	228,916
Gas – other (GWh)	5680	41	235,428
Travel by car (passenger '000 km/yr)	2,406,250	0.056	134,669
Travel by bus (passenger '000 km/yr)	145,406	0.025	3611
Travel by train (passenger '000 km/yr)	145,406	0.031	4452
Travel by air (passenger '000 km/yr)	1,111,350	0.053	58,381
Road freight ('000 tonnes km/yr)	7,308,000	0.098	713,383
Rail freight ('000 tonne km/yr)	55,770	0.017	959
Food (t)	217,290	2.15	466,663
Wood products (m^3 WRME)	520,000	0.97	504,863
Built land (ha)	37,400	2.83	105,964
Recycled waste– glass (t)	3649	0.60	2175
Recycled waste – paper and card (t)	5236	2.04	10,704
Recycled waste – metals (t)	2526	0.25	640
Recycled waste – compost (t)	2569	1.07	2760
Recycled – other domestic (t)	275	1.95	535
Waste – household (t)	252,000	3.16	796,455
Waste – commercial (paper, metal etc) (t)	324,000	2.76	895,330
Waste – inert (brick, concrete etc) (t)	760,000	0.08	62,492
Water – household (m^3)	30,815,125	0.000197	6083

Ecological footprint of Oxfordshire (hectares)			**4,100,000**
Population of Oxfordshire			550,000
Average ecological footprint (hectares per capita)			**7.5**

Note: Conversion factors used are already adjusted for equivalence and in places vary slightly from those given in Chapter 5 due to local adjustments or historical data variations. Results expressed in world average productive space. The built land figure refers to the area 'permanently' appropriated. Adjusted to remove double-counting

Table 8.3 *Consumption–land-use Matrix for the Average Citizen of Santiago (ha)*

	Fossil energy	Built-up area	Arable	Pasture	Forest	Sea	Total
Food	0.11		0.35	0.75		0.24	1.45
Vegetarian	Unknown		0.32				0.32
Animal products	Unknown			0.75		0.24	0.99
Water			0.03				
Housing and furniture	0.04	0.01			0.11		0.16
Transport	0.25	0.00			0.04		0.29
Road	0.18						0.18
Rail	0.00						0.00
Air	0.02						0.02
Coastal/ waterways	0.04						0.04
Goods	0.43	0.00	0.15	0.07	0.09		0.74
Paper production	0.18				0.09		0.27
Clothes (non-synthetic)	0.00		0.02	0.07			0.08
Tobacco			0.13				0.13
Others	0.25						0.25
Total	**0.83**	**0.02**	**0.49**	**0.82**	**0.24**	**0.24**	**2.64**

Total footprint for Santiago:
4,756,000 (population) * 2.64 ha = c12,600,000

tion patterns for a Santiago resident. To give several examples, food consumption was assumed to be proportional to purchasing power (with an adjustment made for the higher price of food within the city); share of the national transport footprint was assumed to be in proportion to vehicle ownership and paper consumption was estimated from the amount found in the municipal waste.

The combination of local and national consumption data provided sufficient resolution to estimate a total and average per capita footprint for Santiago de Chile. Clearly, a more detailed ecological footprint calculation would have been possible had more local data been available.

Table 8.4 *Footprint Distribution in Santiago According to Economic Levels (ha per person)*

	Lowest 10%	Lowest 20%	Second quintile	Third quintile	Fourth quintile	Highest 20%	Highest 10%
Consumption compared to national average (%)	14	18	33	55	91	305	461
Land-based footprint (ha per person)	0.4	0.5	0.9	1.4	2.4	8.0	12.0

Note: This table shows that the average person in the fourth quintile[14] (60 per cent of the population are poorer, 20 per cent of the population are richer) would earn (or spend) 91 per cent of the average income, resulting in a footprint of 2.4 ha per person. The highest 10 per cent have a footprint larger than the average American; the lowest quintile have a footprint smaller than the average Bangladeshi.

DISTRIBUTING IMPACTS

Of course, not everybody in Santiago has the same size of footprint. Using distribution statistics published by the World Bank it is possible to explore how the size of footprint might vary across the population. One crude assumption is that the distribution of footprint within the country is proportional to a person's purchasing power. Even though money flows are rarely correlated with quality of life, as pointed out extensively by the literature criticizing Gross National Product (GNP),[12] they are closely linked to resource flows.[13] Still, these income distribution measures underestimate the gap between rich and poor as various income benefits of the wealthy are hidden and escape most statistical measurement attempts. These hidden benefits include capital gains, savings abroad or informal activities of the wealthy. On the other hand, monetary spending may exaggerate differences in footprint size: typically, additional income may lead to a shift from quantity (or resource-intensive products) to more quality (or labour intensive) goods and services. Table 8.4 shows the resulting land footprint distribution.

ISLAND STATE – FOOTPRINTING GUERNSEY

The easiest geographical region to footprint is probably an island, because its resource and waste flows are clear.

In 1998 John Barrett, of the Environmental Planning Research Unit at John Moores University, Liverpool, calculated the footprint of the small island of Guernsey, one of the Channel Islands between southern

England and northern France. The island is a Crown Dependency of the UK – it has its own Parliament and can make its own laws, but there are close administrative ties with the UK mainland. It covers just 63 km^2 and has a population of 60,000.

The aim was to identify key sustainability issues and formulate recommendations for policy and practice to implement the main goals to achieve sustainability, within a regional context.

There are many compelling, intriguing and practical reasons to study Guernsey:

- Guernsey has an extremely affluent population, with a per capita GNP greater than that of the US, France, Germany and the UK.
- The island's economy is grounded in the financial sector, with this single industry contributing to more than 50 per cent of export value, although agriculture, tourism and other industries also make a significant contribution.
- The Guernsey Parliament has signed no environmental international agreements and is exempt from all European environmental policy.
- As a self-governing island it is acutely aware of its own ecological limits. There is mounting concern over energy use, the security of the water supply and the use of private vehicles.

Data were supplied by the State of Guernsey Engineering Department and a footprint calculated using the same tabular format as employed in the 'Footprint of Nations' study. Table 8.5 displays a simplified version of the spreadsheet. The calculation consists of a consumption analysis of over 120 categories of primary production and manufactured goods. Guernsey imports all its energy (mainly oil). These imports are recorded, providing an adequate measure of energy consumption. The footprint of fossil-fuel consumption is calculated from CO_2 absorption of immature forests.

The rows in Table 8.5 represent the different resource types while the columns contain the yield (kg/ha/yr), import, consumption, embodied energy and the footprint component.[15]

Table 8.6 displays the results of the ecological footprint calculation for Guernsey.

Guernsey Islanders Wear Big Shoes

Guernsey has a large ecological footprint with very little regional biocapacity to offset its resource consumption. The island's footprint spreads well beyond its administrative boundaries.

The per capita footprint is 8.6 hectares, putting Guernsey near the top of the league table of nations, well ahead of major Western European countries. Each islander would appear to be appropriating

Table 8.5 *Extract from the Ecological Footprint Spreadsheet for Guernsey (annual consumption)*

Categories	Global yield	Energy intensity	Import	Apparent consumption	Net trade	Footprint	Land type	Embodied energy in net import	Footprint in import
Units if not specified	(Kg/ha/yr)	(Gj/t)	(t)	(t)	(t)	(ha per cap)		(Pj)	(ha per cap)
Animal-based food products									
Living animals	72.08	5.00	29.00	29.20	29.00	0.01	Pasture	0.00	0.01
Beef (fresh and frozen)	31.99	80.00	16.00	16.00		0.01	Pasture	0.00	0.01
Game		80.00	21.00	21.00					
Pigs and chicken			26.00	26.00					
Other meat	375.92	80.00	1694.90	1694.90	1694.90	0.08	Arable	0.14	0.08
Milk	489.26	10.00	6921.83	6921.83		0.24	Pasture	0.07	0.24
Cheese	48.93	65.00	2039.33	2039.33	2039.33	0.71	Pasture	0.13	0.71
Fish	28.93	100.00	2369.00	2396.00		1.41	Sea	0.24	1.40
Animal-based products									
Wool	15.99	10.00	9.47	9.47		0.01	Pasture	0.00	0.01
Shoes	31.99	20.00	164.22		164.22	0.09	Pasture	0.00	0.09
Animal raw materials	72.08	10.00	45.33		45.33	0.01	Pasture	0.00	0.01
Plant-based food									
Corn	4136.00	10.00	3496.00	3496.00	3496.00	0.01	Arable	0.03	0.01
Vegetables (prepared)	18,000.00	20.00	2554.53		2554.53	0.00	Arable	0.05	0.00
Fruit	12,000.00	10.00	730.63	730.63		0.00	Arable	0.01	0.00

Energy balance

Global average (Gj/ha/yr)	Footprint component in (ha per cap)
55.00	0.16 Fossil energy land for coal
71.00	1.45 Fossil energy land (liquid fuel)
93.00	0.09 Fossil energy land (fossil gas)
71.00	3.17 Fossil energy land for embodied energy in net imported goods

Table 8.6 *Summary of the Guernsey Ecological Footprint Calculation*[16]

Category	Total (ha per cap)	Equivalence factor	Equivalent total (ha per cap)
Fossil energy	4.87	1.17	5.69
Arable land	0.35	2.83	0.99
Pasture	1.09	0.44	0.48
Forest	0.74	1.17	0.87
Built-up area	0.17	2.83	0.48
Sea	1.45	0.06	0.09
Total			**8.6**

more than four times the average earthshare of resources, although approximately 0.5 ha per capita is thought to be due to the activity of tourists, who should more correctly bear the responsibility for this impact.[17] Therefore Guernsey islanders not only wear very big shoes, but are almost entirely dependent on appropriating the bio-productivity outside of their borders.

In the words of John Barrett, Guernsey 'defies the laws of natural carrying capacity' to a generous degree. Were it not for the ease with which it can trade on the global market, Guernsey would indeed be Europe's own Easter Island.[18]

NOTES

1   William Rees, 'Is "Sust City" an Oxymoron?' in *Local Environment*, vol 2, no 3, 1997, pp303–310
2   This trend has been observed by the authors in the USA and UK. In other countries, such as Portugal, an influx of large food retailers has tended to lead to the decline of established fresh food markets
3   For example, Herbert Girardet produced a short TV series in 1996 on the metabolism of London for Channel 4 in the UK. There is also a comprehensive manifesto for a Sustainable London: http://www.greenchannel.com/slt/substant.htm, and the London Research Centre's 'London Energy Study' prepared under the Commission of the European Communities' Urban and Regional Energy Management Programme, 1993
4   http://www.denhaag.nl (last accessed 5/11/99). Information kindly supplied by Theo Breumelhof, City Management Department, The Hague Town Hall, F0818, PO Box 12651, NL 2500 DP, The Hague, Holland
5   'Ecosystem Appropriation by Cities', Folke, C, Jansson, A, Larsson, J and Costanza, R, *Ambio*, vol 26, no 3, May 1997
6   Only phosphorous and nitrogen from human waste was considered. Other sources – food processing, household waste, car emissions and so on – were not included

7   The authors remain cautious about methods of accounting for waste. It is all too easy to 'double count' land – for example, counting arable land twice for both food production and phosphorous assimilation. Although the assimilation of wastes, other than carbon, is clearly an omission in our current footprinting methodology, we prefer to understate the footprint by continuing to omit them until we have devised a comprehensive means by which they can be included. The Sustainable Process Index (see Box 10.2) has made some headway with the footprinting of wastes and our own tentative first steps are presented in Chapter 10, where we look at comparing different packaging materials

8   For more information about the Stepwise service see the BFF web site: http://www.bestfootforward.com

9   Various sources were used including data from Transco (gas company), Southern Electric, Oxfordshire County Council, Regional Trends 32 (Office of National Statistics), Berkshire, Buckinghamshire, Oxfordshire Wildlife Trust (BBONT) (a local wildlife group). Local data for wood and food were not available so these were estimated from national sources.

10 Oxfordshire has a land area of 270,000 hectares and a population of around 550,000. About 80 per cent of Oxfordshire is designated as either an Area of Outstanding Natural Beauty (AONB), an Area of High Landscape Value (AHLV) or Green Belt and it could reasonably be argued that this area should be treated specially. Certainly, these areas have varying degrees of protection under law, which restricts the use to which they can be put. Britain has approximately 20,500,000 hectares of land and 58 million inhabitants

11 Wackernagel, M, 1998, 'The Ecological Footprint of Santiago de Chile', *Local Environment*, vol 3, no 2

12 For example, see Herman Daly and John Cobb's discussion in *For the Common Good*, 1989, Beacon Press, Boston

13 For example, see Charles A S Hall, Cutler J Cleveland and Robert Kaufmann, 1986, *Energy and Resource Quality*, John Wiley & Sons, New York

14 A quintile is one fifth or 20 per cent

15 Usually, a footprint measurement would include local production and exports. In the case of Guernsey it was decided that these were so minimal that they should not be included. The only measurements for the footprint are based on imports to the island

16 The same equivalence factors are used as in the 'Footprint of Nations' study

17 Personal discussions with John Barrett

18 As this book went to press, Best Foot Forward were completing a study of the Isle of Wight. The report, 'Island State', will be made available at http://www.ecological.footprint.com

Chapter 9

Assessing the Impact of Organizations and Services

'The language of commerce sounds specific, but in fact it is not explicit enough. If Hawaiians had 138 different ways to describe falling rain, we can assume that rain had a profound importance in their lives. Business, on the other hand, only has two words for profit – gross and net...(they make) no distinctions as to how the profit was made' (Paul Hawken, 1994)

There are sound reasons why an organization, whether it is a private company, public or voluntary body, would wish to reduce their impact on the environment and become more 'eco-efficient'. As the World Business Council on Sustainable Development (WBCSD) points out, 'Eco-efficiency can help create value for the company and society as a whole by explicitly promoting change toward sustainable growth. This emphasis on creating and adding value is clearly to society's benefit.'[1] The carrot of increased resource efficiency and its associated financial benefits, as well as company image and the push of legislation, is causing organizations to seek ways to measure their eco-efficiency.

While the WBCSD also defines eco-efficiency as '...progressively reducing ecological impacts and resource intensity throughout the life cycle, to a level at least in line with the earth's estimated carrying capacity', as yet it provides no framework to assess this. Ecological footprinting, with its feet squarely planted in carrying capacity, has considerable potential to provide this framework.

As we saw in Chapter 2, we can do this using life cycle analysis data. If, for example, we are able to attribute an ecological footprint value to a product or service, we can then start to estimate its contribution to carrying capacity. We can also do this by looking at organizational performance data and expressing it per unit of product or service.

In addition, EFA provides the opportunity for benchmarking of organizational environmental performance. Relatively recently we have seen the advent of 'league tables' of corporate environmental performance, such as the Business in the Environment Index of Corporate Engagement.[2] However, as its name suggests, this only assesses management performance – such as the existence of a policy statement or whether the organization produces an environmental report. Benchmarking of actual environmental performance is currently hindered by the fact that few organizations measure energy use and fewer still measure material flows. Until such data collection becomes standard practice, performance benchmarking will be limited; and when it becomes standard practice, EFA will provide an excellent method for presenting those benchmarks.

WEBBED FEET

Best Foot Forward was approached by Anglian Water Services (AWS), a utility interested in understanding and reducing its impact on the environment. The utility was primarily concerned with the relative significance of its transport, waste and energy use, and its interest extended to future energy policy scenarios and the use of footprinting as a projection tool. Table 9.1 presents the data provided by the company on current consumption (1997 was the most recent available) along with footprint conversions.

Based on the assumptions given, the total footprint for 1997 consumption was calculated as 158,200 ha. As we can see, the main impacts arose from grid electricity and general office waste. Without further data on the waste streams it was not possible to footprint the latter more accurately and one recommendation was to put more effort into tracking material flows through the organization.

Normalizing this footprint figure by the amount of water delivered gives us some valuable insights. Firstly, we can estimate per capita or household footprint values attributable to water supply. For example, in 1997 the company delivered 360,000 Ml to a population of four million customers in 1.77 million properties, an average of 90,000 litres per person or 203,390 litres per property. The footprint per Ml for 1997 is $158,200/360,000 = 0.44$ ha. So we can derive a footprint figure of 0.089 ha per property per year.

Secondly, normalization of this nature enables us to estimate eco-efficiency and investigate scenarios to improve it.

Considering this, and the fact that energy use was a significant contributor to the footprint value, a second recommendation to the water utility was to look in more detail at energy consumption. This was well documented, and of considerable concern, given the clear trend towards increasing demand. The company had plans in place to

Table 9.1 *Footprint of Selected Activities: Anglian Water Services*

Activity (per year)	1997 data	Footprint conversion	Footprint (ha)
Transport ('000 km – diesel)	52,170	0.08	3964
Waste (tonnes of spoil)[a]	604,000	0.004	2612
Waste (tonnes of office waste)[b]	36,000	2.54	91,418
Short Rotation Coppicing (MWh)[c]	0	0.012	0
Wind Energy – (MWh)	0	0.006	0
Grid Electricity (MWh)[d]	544,500	0.11	60,215
Biogas (MWh)[e]	60,500	0	0
Total (rounded to nearest 100 ha)			**158,200**

Notes:
a This is mostly soil moved in the process of digging. The footprint conversion factor is based on the embodied energy to extract sand and gravel (ETSU 1994 report B/W5/00337/REP 'Modelling of Carbon and Energy Budgets of Wood Fuel Coppice Systems')
b Office waste is assumed to be 70 per cent paper, 30 per cent plastics
c Data based on the exploratory work for an SRC-fuelled combined heat and power (CHP) plant undertaken by Yorkshire Water in the UK (Personal communication, Next Step Consulting)
d Based on energy generation in the UK, which includes a large portion of gas
e A decision was made that, as far as this organization was concerned, the footprint of biogas derived from sewage sludge was effectively zero. It depends, of course, on where one draws the boundaries. One could – if one was so minded – calculate the land required for the food input necessary to produce the sludge. It was felt that this was unnecessarily 'lavatorial'

invest in renewable energy technologies and was interested to analyse the impacts of possible energy scenarios.

Various scenarios were explored and the favoured one considered alongside best estimates of rising demand and various energy-saving ideas. Table 9.2 sets out the data for this scenario at seven-year intervals to 2011. As can be seen, the demand for grid electricity is predicted to rise – due mainly to the imminent arrival of more stringent water processing standards – although some of this is offset by increased use of wind, biogas and biomass.

Table 9.3 sets out the footprint data for Table 9.2. These figures assume that no fundamental changes in technology occur, for example, in the efficiency of energy production.

As can be seen from the totals, the environmental benefits of switching to renewable forms of energy – and the other savings – were insufficient to counter the predicted rise in the use of fossil fuels – the main source of grid electricity.

However, over the period of the projection it was believed that the company customer base and increasing demand would increase the

Table 9.2 *Consumption Data – Projection in Seven-year Intervals for Favoured Scenario*

Activity	1997 data	2004 data	2011 data
Transport ('000 km – diesel)	52,170	46,953	46,953
Waste (tonnes of spoil)	604,000	348,360	348,360
Waste (office waste – mostly paper)	36,000	36,000	36,000
Short rotation coppicing (MWh)	0	49,275	57,050
Wind Energy (MWh)	0	19,710	22,820
Grid Electricity (MWh)	544,500	615,937	713,125
Biogas (MWh)	60,500	172,463	199,675

amount of water distribution by about 20 per cent. Any measure of eco-efficiency should take into account this change. Assuming that a figure of 360,000 Ml/year of water was distributed in 1997 and 400,000 Ml/year in 2011, calculating eco-efficiency per delivered megalitre year gives a footprint of 0.44 ha, falling to 0.42 ha over the period in question. Thus some degree of improvement in eco-efficiency can be discerned.

Thus EFA proved to be a helpful tool in this instance, accepting that projections were necessarily based on current technologies.

UNIVERSITY CHALLENGE

A similar analysis can be applied to service-based organizations. In 1998, Best Foot Forward produced a computer-based footprint calculator as part of a university campaign being run by People & Planet – a UK non-governmental organization.[3] The software, called 'Campus-Calc' (see Figure 9.2), has been supplied to student groups throughout the UK and allows them to derive an ecological footprint for their university campus.

A CampusCalc analysis considers the key areas of travel, energy, waste, paper and water use. Information is also supplied on student numbers and turnover. Both of these are used to normalize the footprint value to express it as an eco-efficiency indicator.

To put this in context, the use of CampusCalc is illustrated below, using data for Oxford Brookes University kindly supplied by Kevin Paulson, formerly a member of the Brookes Environment Forum.[4]

Oxford Brookes is a growing university situated in Headington, in the city of Oxford, England. It has approximately 1500 staff and 13,000 students. The main campuses of Gypsy Lane and Headington Hill cover an area of 11 ha sandwiched between residential and parkland to the

Table 9.3 *Footprint Analysis Results Projection in Seven-year Intervals*

Activity	1997 (ha)	2004 (ha)	2011 (ha)
Transport	3964	3568	3568
Waste – spoil	2612	1506	1506
Waste – office waste	91,418	91,418	91,418
Short rotation coppicing	0	605	700
Wind energy	0	119	138
Grid electricity	60,215	59,968	69,430
Biogas	0	0	0
Totals (rounded to nearest 100 ha)	**158,200**	**157,200**	**166,800**

east of the city centre. The larger out-of-town campus of Wheatley Park covers 21 ha.

Consumption data were obtained from either official university sources or, in the case of travel, from research by the university's own planning department.

Data for transport, energy and paper use are summarized in Table 9.4. Footprint conversion factors are taken from the earlier chapter. It should be noted that no data were available for student commuting. This was estimated, based on a figure of 30 per cent car ownership and journeys averaging 15 km per day for 150 days per year.

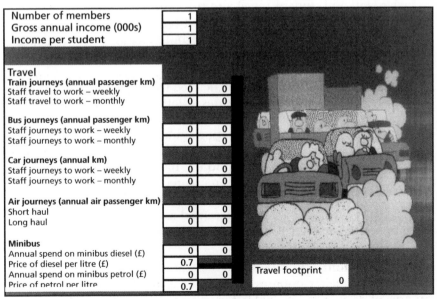

Figure 9.2 *Screen-shot of CampusCalc*

Table 9.4 *Oxford Brookes University – Summary Data and Footprint Analysis*

Annual impact data	Value (unit)	Conversion factor (ha-year per unit)	Footprint (ha)
Staff journeys to university ('000 car km/year)	6280	0.09	562
Student journeys to university (estimated '000 car km/year)	8775	0.09	786
Business flights by staff ('000 passenger km/year)	5211	0.08	417
Gas consumption 1996 (GWh/year)	7.7	45.3	349
Electricity consumption 1996 (GWh/year)	4.4	110.60	487
Paper consumption (t/year)	116.25	1.88	219
Total			**2819**

The total footprint of around 2800 hectares is about 80 times the size of the Brookes campus. It can be seen that the largest impacts arise from daily commuting and electricity consumption, although other consumption data are also significant. If commuting and business flights are combined, then the travel footprint is by far the largest.

As a result of the study, the university considered the urgent need to tackle staff and student travel and this resulted in the production of a green commuter plan.[5] This included targets for traffic reduction, establishment of new public transport routes, more video-conferencing, charging for parking permits and the removal of on-site car parking spaces.

Eco-efficiency indicators can be derived by comparing the footprint with any one of a number of measures – staff and student numbers and revenue are the most obvious choices. If we are trying to assess the creation of value, in this case educating students, footprint per full-time equivalent student is perhaps the most appropriate. A per-student footprint would work out at around 0.2 ha per year – 2819/13,000 = 0.22 ha inclusive of all the impacts measured.

In this example, as the data provided focus on staff travel, the footprint per member of staff is presented as an example. This is calculated (for travel only) as 979/1500 = 0.65 ha per year.

Box 9.1 Greening Education: An Ecological Footprint of Ryde School[6]

Ryde School on the Isle of Wight, off the south coast of England, occupies 7.3 hectares. It is attended by a total of 815 people, including teachers, pupils and service staff. The school is keenly active on environmental issues and kindly provided Best Foot Forward with detailed consumption data including:

- direct energy use
- transport
- material consumption
- waste production
- water use

Data were also provided on the purchase of 'long life' goods such as equipment and machinery. As these items have a lifespan of longer than a year, they were treated as 'capital goods' and their impacts discounted over their expected lifespan.

The total ecological footprint of the school was found to be 150 ha, equivalent to 0.22 ha per full-time pupil. This footprint can be accounted for as in the table below. Unfortunately, no data on building were available.

	Components	Footprint (ha)
Throughput:		147.00
of which	Energy	14.82
	Transport	48.13
	Food	53.01
	Materials	30.76
	Waste	0.06
	Water	0.23
Capital goods:		3.38
of which	Buildings	no data
	Goods	3.00
	Other capital goods	0.38
Ecological footprint:	**Total**	**150.38**
of which	**Per pupil**	**0.22**

Previous analyses have found the island's total footprint to be 565,300 ha or 4.5 ha per capita (after adjustment has been made for tourism). The total footprint of the school is therefore equivalent to 0.02 per cent of the total ecological footprint of the Isle of Wight economy and 5 per cent of the per capita footprint.

A similar exercise has been carried out for another school on the UK mainland by Lloyd Lewis Power in Southampton and the Southampton Environment Centre. When equivalent activities were accounted, the footprint of each pupil at this school was 0.31 ha. This is 41 per cent higher than Ryde School's footprint. This is probably indicative of the considerable efforts made by Ryde School to reduce energy usage and waste.

NOTES

1   WBCSD Eco-efficiency Bulletin, January 1999
2   BiE: http://www.business-in-environment.org.uk
3   People and Planet website: http://www.peopleandplanet.org
4   Kevin Paulson (personal communication, 1998) and unpublished draft
     paper 'The Transport Footprint of Oxford Brookes University', 1998
5   'Green Commuter Plan', Oxford Brookes University, 1999
6   Analyses of the Ryde and Mainland schools were undertaken by Best
     Foot Forward. The study of the former is included in the 'Island State'
     report available via http://www.ecologicalfootprint.com

Chapter 10

Footprinting for Product Assessment

'Perhaps society had been looking at materials flows from the wrong end altogether' (Factor Four, 1998)[1]

ECOLOGICAL FOOTPRINTING – ONE STEP ON FROM LIFE CYCLE ASSESSMENT

The last decade has seen an increasing demand for information on the environmental impacts of products, partly to assist designers in 'Design for the Environment' and partly to inform consumers about the relative environmental impacts of purchases. LCA methodologies and weighting schemes such as EcoPoints, referenced in Chapter 2, have arisen primarily as a means of comparing the environmental attributes of one product against another for the purpose of 'green marketing' and eco-labelling. However, as the authors have previously pointed out, 'weighted LCA' information, while providing a single aggregate indicator, does little to identify absolute environmental impact, thereby linking the effects of our use of products to the global availability of resources or sustainability. For example, one washing machine might score 1000 EcoPoints, another model might score 2000, so we can compare the two products. But unless we know how many EcoPoints there are in the world we have no way of estimating the contribution of that product to carrying capacity and therefore sustainability. Ecological footprinting follows the same principles as LCA but does not use subjective weightings. It is therefore able to link product impacts to carrying capacity.

SENSE AND SENSITIVITY

Of all the applications of EFA, product assessment is probably the most experimental. This is in part due to lack of the necessary data on the environmental impacts of products. Until relatively recently, LCA studies of products have been limited. Where they do exist, they are often hotly contested and the sensitivity of the assessments questioned.

The EFA of products is presented here with a 'health warning' – it has traditionally been applied at the macro level where individual behavioural differences and uncertainty about minor data (for example whether items are recycled or thrown away) become less significant. While the use of EFA to measure resource use is well tried, the conversion of some pollutants to their land-area equivalents is still uncommon. This is mainly due to problems of system complexity and data availability. Nonetheless, a number of studies have been published which provide enough credible data to perform a basic pollution analysis. To enhance the accuracy of EFA for products, items with in-depth life cycle inventory data have been chosen. Outlined below are two analyses of products. The first, on various nappy systems (or diapers, as they are referred to in the USA), was carried out in 1996 and focuses primarily on resource usage. The second, on drinks containers systems, was carried out in 1999 after further development of the methodology and looks additionally at the ecological footprints of pollutants.

Uses case studies e-g nappia.

NAPPIES – THE SINGLE BOTTOM LINE

In the process of developing 'EcoCal', the household ecological footprinting tool, nappy use was identified as a significant issue. Because the environmental impact of different types of nappy has been vigorously debated between manufacturers and environmentalists, several LCA studies have been carried out and data are relatively easily available.

The most recent comprehensive study is the Canadian work by Vizcarra,[2] commissioned in 1995 by Procter and Gamble. Our analysis is based on these data as they are generally regarded as the most credible.

The analysis is conducted on the basis of impact per baby year. The study compares the ecological footprint of disposable nappies, home-laundered reusable nappies and service-laundered nappies. The Vizcarra study uses Canadian data, which are likely to be similar for any industrialized nation.

Table 10.1 summarizes the life cycle inventory data for the three types of service and a range of footprint values. All are expressed as hectares 'per baby year'.

The data used in an EFA of any product are subject to variability both at the life cycle inventory stage and in the conversion to footprint

Table 10.1 *Annual Resource Use for Nappies, with Ecological Footprint Conversion Figures*

Resource	EF conversion values – low	EF conversion values – high	Disposables			Reusables – home laundered			Reusables – service laundered		
			Value	EF – low (ha)	EF – high (ha)	Value	EF – low (ha)	EF – high (ha)	Value	EF – low (ha)	EF – high (ha)
Energy – manufacture	0.0164 ha/GJ	0.0270 ha/GJ	8.216GJ	0.135	0.222	0.832GJ	0.014	0.023	1.768GJ	0.029	0.048
Energy – use			0.000GJ	0.000	0.000	8.788GJ	0.145	0.238	4.888GJ	0.080	0.132
Water – manufacture	0.0002 ha/m³	0.0009 ha/m³	21.580m³	0.004	0.020	8.008 m³	0.002	0.008	10.970m³	0.002	0.010
Water – use			0.000m³	0.000	0.000	41.650m³	0.008	0.039	17.060m³	0.003	0.016
Paper	0.0019 ha/kg	0.0035 ha/kg	159.640kg	0.300	0.558	0.000kg	0.000	0.000	0.000kg	0.000	0.000
Cotton	0.0033 ha/kg	0.0058 ha/kg	–	0.000	0.000	2.600kg	0.009	0.015	4.160kg	0.014	0.024
Total				**0.44**	**0.80**		**0.18**	**0.32**		**0.13**	**0.23**

Note: All figures are based on one baby year. Cotton conversion values differ from those in Chapter 5 as they are based on the life cycle of raw, rather than finished, materials.

LIVERPOOL JOHN MOORES UNIVERSITY
LEARNING SERVICES

values. For example, for nappies, energy consumption per baby year can vary according to wash-water temperatures or efficiency of service laundries.[3]

In addition there can be variability in the footprint conversion values used. For example, we use a footprint conversion value of 0.0164 hectare years per GJ if energy for manufacture is derived directly from oil or 0.0270 hectare years per GJ if it is derived from electricity. The conversion value for paper varies depending on processing energy of paper and the conversion value for cotton varies according to yield factors in the field. Conversion values for water depend on the embodied energy of water delivered, which will depend on things like efficiency of treatment and distribution.

The analysis indicates the lower environmental impact of reusable nappy systems. Of the two reusable systems, the service-laundered nappies appear to be the best choice based on the life cycle assumptions made. Summary results are presented in Figure 10.2.

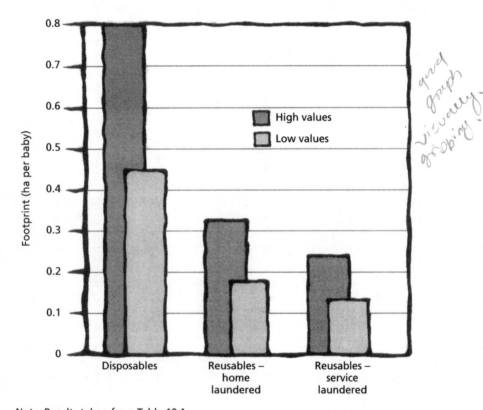

Note: Results taken from Table 10.1

Figure 10.2 *Ecological footprint values for three nappy systems*

BOTTLES AND CANS

*questions
are new as
re ahat here.*

At the request of the European Green Group, and sponsored by the Dutch GreenLeft, Best Foot Forward carried out an EFA of a number of different drinks packaging systems based on the LCA data collected and collated by the Danish Environmental Protection Agency.[4]

The LCA studies considered a range of production, energy, transport and waste disposal and recycling scenarios before deciding on the assumptions most appropriate and realistic for Denmark. For example, their scenarios assumed high levels of packaging reuse and recycling.

Packaging can be responsible for far more environmental damage than the product itself. Box 10.1 documents the travels of a can of cola.

We present two sets of results based on two different approaches to the modelling of pollution within the context of an EFA. The first method (EF I) uses conversion factors under development by Best Foot Forward as part of their EcoIndex measurement system. The second (EF II) uses values developed for the Sustainable Process Index (SPI) by the University of Graz in Austria (see Box 10.2).

The second method results in larger footprints for two reasons. Firstly, a less conservative approach is taken in calculating the 'damage' caused by pollution. Rather than adopting the concept of 'critical loads' to measure damage – the method used by the authors for compatibility with current footprint resource accounting calculations – the SPI method uses natural flows of materials as criteria for sustainability. The effect of this is both to increase the magnitude of impacts and, to a lesser extent, emphasize different pollutants. Secondly, the SPI method of area accounting is additive, thereby increasing the likelihood of the 'double counting' of impacts. Thus, the EF II method both imposes stricter sustainability criteria and cannot readily be used to relate impact to local or global carrying capacity. Box 10.2 gives a fuller explanation of the SPI method. Although EF II will, by definition, always indicate a larger impact than EF I, it is the relative impact of the different packaging systems that is of most interest.

Refreshing Results

The results from any study of this nature need to be treated with some caution. No methodology is perfect – each has its strengths and weaknesses – and this is equally true with EFA, where the measurement of pollution is problematic due in part to a lack of robust research. A particular note of caution is expressed with regard to the categories of waste identified in the Danish study as 'hazardous', 'slag and ashes', and 'nuclear'. These are not currently included in the EcoIndex methodology and were therefore excluded from the analysis.

This study demonstrates the complexity of impact assessment and shows how a whole range of variables in the lifecycle, as well as the EFA

Box 10.1 Cola Travels

The packaging of items for transport can lead to significant environmental impacts. Take, for example, a can of cola for consumption in the UK. The can is much more costly and complex to manufacture than the beverage. Bauxite is mined in Australia, taken to a mill and purified into aluminium oxide. It is then taken by ship to Scandinavia where it is smelted into aluminium metal. It is then shipped again, possibly to Germany, where it is rolled into aluminium sheet. The material is then shipped once again to England where it is formed into cans which are washed, treated and painted. The completed cans, still empty, are then warehoused until required.

In contrast, the cola drink, is made from water and flavoured syrup, derived from French sugar beet, American mined phosphorus and chemically-derived caffeine.

The canned drink is then further packaged and distributed to regional warehouses and individual stores, before being purchased by the consumer.

One brief, refreshing, drink later the can – more often than not – ends up in a landfill site. In the UK only 36 per cent of aluminium cans are recycled.

Source: Womack and Jones,[5] APRO[6]

---

method used, can influence the final result. It is interesting though that all three methods, including the original LCA study, show a remarkable degree of consistency in the ranking of the packaging systems. As explained earlier, one would not expect the scale of impacts to be the same given the differing system criteria employed to assess pollution.

A full discussion of the variations is outside the scope of this book, but suffice to say the key differences in magnitude between the EF I and EF II methods were due, in particular, to their treatment of SO_2 and NO_x emissions.[7]

Table 10.2 shows the results for the various container systems, using the two different methods. All results are rounded up to the nearest square metre.

For 25 and 33 cl containers, the glass packaging systems (both disposable and refillable) have a lower footprint than the aluminium and steel packaging systems although the difference between disposable green glass (33 cl) and aluminium (33 cl) is small.

For the 50 cl and 150 cl packaging systems, the analyses indicate a clear 'leader' – the refillable polyethylene terephthalate plastic (PET) containers, the material is that usually used for large fizzy drink bottles.

In the assessment of the 50 cl packaging systems (disposable PET, steel and aluminium cans) the differences in approach between the EF I and EF II methods are most apparent. In particular, disposable PET is ranked last with EF II and second with EF I. This can be traced to the

Table 10.2 *Comparison of the Ecological Footprints of Different Packaging Systems*

System:	Footprint per 1000 litres EF I $(m^2$-year$)$[8]	Footprint per 1000 litres EF II $(m^2$-year$)$
25 & 33 cl		
Refillable glass – 33 cl green	1535 [1]	10,887 [1]
Disposable glass – 33 cl clear	1653 [2]	19,921 [3]
Refillable glass – 25 cl clear	1703 [3]	12,436 [2]
Disposable glass – 33 cl green	2014 [4]	21,775 [4]
Aluminium cans – 33 cl	2514 [5]	22,134 [5]
Steel cans – 33 cl	3898 [6]	27,804 [6]
50 cl		
Refillable PET	489 [1]	7392 [1]
Disposable PET	1496 [2]	28,391 [4]
Aluminium cans	1994 [3]	17,837 [2]
Steel cans	3945 [4]	21,714 [3]
150 cl		
Refillable PET	388 [1]	6043 [1]
Disposable PET	799 [2]	16,596 [2]

Note: Rankings appear in square brackets – 1 is best, 6 is worst. Table is split to distinguish different container sizes. High levels of can recycling are assumed

high levels of SO_2 and NO_x emissions resulting from the use of disposable PET bottles.

PRODUCTS AND SUSTAINABILITY

Each of the analyses presented here serves two purposes. Firstly, they demonstrate how EFA can be used as an index of impact for comparing what are essentially two different services – baby hygiene and drinks delivery. Secondly, and perhaps more enlightening, they provide a means of linking product and service use with environmental sustainability. For example, if an individual drinks the UK average of 75 litres of soft drinks a year, and we assume that this was delivered in 50 cl steel

Box 10.2 The Sustainable Process Index[9]

The SPI, originally developed at the University of Graz in Austria, is an area-based index similar to the ecological footprint. Its purpose is to analyse and compare the overall ecological impact of industrial processes and, more generally, human activities. The method adds up the land area required to provide resources and to assimilate emissions and waste that are generated in the process of delivering a service. The SPI includes the following components:

$$A_{tot} = AR + AE + AI + AS + AP$$

where AR is the area required to produce raw materials, AE the area to provide process energy, AI the area to provide the equipment for the process, AS the area required for staff, and AP the areas to accommodate products and by-products (including emissions and waste). All are measured in m^2.

Note that the SPI accounts for areas used in the past (temporal shift in the case of fossil materials or aquifers) and for areas borrowed from the future (temporal shift of highly polluted areas with a long regeneration gap). These past and future footprints are dominating the picture of today's state-of-the-art technologies, as has been shown in numerous SPI case studies.

While ecological footprints only account for basic and spatially segregated ecological impacts, the SPI applies stricter sustainability criteria and includes more impacts than footprinting presently does. SPI builds its assessments on the premises that:

- Anthropogenic material flows must not exceed the local assimilation capacity and should be smaller than the fluctuations of naturally occurring flows of these substances.
- Anthropogenic material flows must not alter the quality and the quantity of global material cycles. Renewable resources can only be extracted at a rate that does not exceed the local fertility.
- The natural variety of species and landscapes must be sustained or improved.

These criteria are similar to the principals (or 'system conditions') of 'The Natural Step' originally proposed by Karl-Henrik Robèrt and his colleagues (see Box 2.2). In the SPI concept these sustainability criteria are used in an 'evaluation procedure' where material flows, induced by human activities, are compared with 'natural' material flows (generation and degeneration rates). If we compare this approach to the policy approach of 'critical loads', where the absorptive capacity of land is defined for various pollutants, SPI assumes stricter sustainability criteria.

However, since some of the ecological functions adding up to the SPI do not mutually exclude each other, the SPI, unlike the footprint, does not document which portion of the biosphere's capacity is appropriated for a given human-made process. And it does this on purpose for the following benefit. This 'double-counting' makes the SPI measure more sensitive to improvements of a process. In contrast, footprints only change if primary ecological functions are affected. While the footprint shows whether society is meeting the overall condition of being within the ecological capacity, the SPI offers a directional measure about how much processes are improving their ecological performance.

Contributed by Christian Krotscheck of the Kronberg Institute.

cans, we can estimate the ecological footprint of the containers as nearly 300m². If we assume an average sustainable global per capita earthshare of 1.8 ha, then soft drinks consumption would appear to 'use up' about 1.7 per cent of this. We could also usefully compare drinks consumption with other activities – such as car travel. The average European citizen drives around 10,500 km a year. The corresponding footprint value is in the region of 6600 m², representing 37 per cent of the average earthshare – 20 times the impact of drinking.

So, although the methodology needs further development in terms of data integrity and standardized treatment of pollution loads, even in its present state it can provide an insight into product use, sustainability and where we might want to target our improvement efforts.

NOTES

1   Weizsäcker, E, Lovins, A, and Lovins, L H, *Factor Four – Doubling wealth halving resource use*, Earthscan, 1998
2   Vizcarra, A T, Lo K V and Liao, P H, 'A Life Cycle Inventory of Baby Diapers Subject to Canadian Conditions', in *Environmental Toxicology and Chemistry*, vol 13, no 10, pp1707–1716, 1994
3   See Vizcarra, op cit, for sensitivity analysis of LCI data
4   Ekvall et al, op cit, 1998, Environmental Project No 399, Danish Environmental Protection Agency
5   Womack, J P and Jones, D T *Lean Thinking: Banish Waste and Create Wealth in Your Corporation*, Simon and Schuster, New York, 1996
6   Aluminium Packaging Recycling Organisation, Birmingham, UK. Data for 1998, personal communication, November 1999. Encouragingly, the figure has increased from only 2 per cent in 1989
7   For further information the reader is directed to the original report (http://www.ecologicalfootprint.com) and the work of Christian Krotscheck (see previous note)
8   EF I is used as this is most comparable with the ecological footprinting method used elsewhere in this book
9   Krotscheck, C and Narodoslawsky, M, 1996, 'The Sustainable Process Index – A new Dimension in Ecological Evaluation', *Ecological Engineering*, vol 6, no 4, pp241–258; Krotscheck, C, 1997, 'How to Measure Sustainability? Comparison of flow-based (mass and/or energy) highly aggregated indicators for eco-compatibility', *EnvironMetrics*, vol 8, pp661–681; Krotscheck, C, 1998, 'Quantifying the Interaction of Human

and the Ecosphere: The Sustainable Process Index as Measure for Co-existence', in Müller, F and Leupelt, M (eds) *Eco-Targets, Goal Functions, and Orientors*, Springer Verlag, Berlin, Heidelberg, New York; web site: http://vt.tu-graz.ac.at/spi/, last accessed 1 December 1999

Chapter 11

Footprinting Lifestyles – How Big is Your Ecological Garden?

'Hoc erat in votis: modus agri non ita magnus, hortus ubi et tecto vicinus iugis aquae fons et paulum silvae super his foret' (This was among my prayers: a piece of land not very large, where a garden should be and a spring of ever flowing water near the house, and a bit of woodland as well as these) Horace (65–8 BC)

DEVELOPING A GREEN HOUSEHOLD INDEX

In 1995 two of the authors (Chambers and Simmons) set to work on a number of prototype software programmes with the aim of making the calculation of footprints less onerous and more accessible to a wider audience. One of these, which had a working title of the Green Household Index, finally saw the light as a fully functioning product in the UK in 1997. Called 'EcoCal', it was developed on behalf of Going for Green by Best Foot Forward.[1]

EcoCal is first and foremost an easy-to-use computer-based questionnaire which combines a footprint-based measurement scheme with a package of facts, hints, tips and contact details aimed at bringing about more environmentally-responsible behaviour (see Figure 11.2). It is designed to be used by the general public. For those without access to a computer, EcoCal is also produced in a paper-based format.

EcoCal enables a household to measure what the authors have termed its 'ecological garden' – the amount of bioproductive space required to support the lifestyles of the occupiers.

For practical reasons, the EcoCal questionnaire comprised just 45 questions. These were organized into six categories of household impact: transport, energy, water, waste, house and garden, and purchas-

Table 11.1 *Overview of Information Gathered by EcoCal*

Category	Information gathered	
Transport	Distance travelled by car	Distance travelled by air
	Distance travelled by bus/train	Number of air trips
Energy	Electricity consumption	Coal consumption
	Gas consumption	LPG consumption
	Oil consumption	
Water	Number of dishwasher runs	Hours of hosepipe use
	Number of washing machine runs	Number of baths and showers
Purchasing	Food purchased – grown in EU	Number of newspapers
	Food purchased – transported by air	Number and type of nappies purchased
	Food purchased – transported by sea	Nights spent in hotel
		Rating of hotel
	Meat products – per cent purchased	
	Organic products – per cent purchased	
House and garden	Size and type of property	Volume of hardwoods purchased
	Volume of peat purchased	Size of plot occupied by property
Waste	Categories of items recycled or composted	Weight of bulk waste produced
	Weight of waste produced	Volume of oil disposed of improperly

ing. Table 11.1 provides an overview of the information gathered within each topic.

Such a short questionnaire cannot hope to measure all impacts. Questions were therefore determined on the basis of availability of data, significance of the impact, and the ability of households to 'make a difference' by acting to reduce their score.

The footprint conversion factors used for the items reported in Table 11.1 were the forerunners of the EcoIndex methodology reported earlier in this book. With the benefit of hindsight, it can be said that the footprint values produced by EcoCal are a conservative underestimate of actual footprints, especially in the categories of waste and water.

HOUSEHOLD FOOTPRINT

During the summer of 1997 'Going for Green' put EcoCal through a rigorous market testing programme, which provided the authors with the opportunity to collect data on the ecological footprints of UK

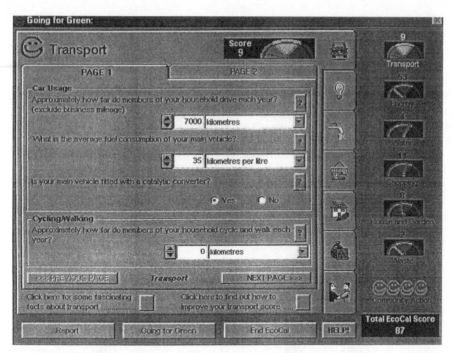

Note: This software is distributed to households in the UK by Going for Green. It is also used for educational purposes by the Open University and by several companies for employee environmental-awareness training.

Figure 11.2 *Screen-shot from EcoCal*

households. The authors were eager to determine both how impacts were distributed across different activities and to explore those aspects of household lifestyles which had the most significant effect.

Data from 42 households (90 adults and about 35 children) were felt reliable enough to be included in our final analysis. These were collected from six regions within the UK, chosen to represent a range of socio-economic factors. Household size varied from one to five adults (aged over 16).

Households were largely self-selecting although a financial incentive was provided to entice the widest cross-section of participants.

The average household ecological footprint was found to be around 3.6 ha or 1.7 ha per adult occupant (1.2 ha including children). It should be noted that this is only part of the total footprint – it cannot be directly compared with the national average data presented in Chapter 7, which are more inclusive. Nonetheless, assuming a typical semi-detached house in the UK occupies a 150 m² plot of land, its 'ecological garden' would then occupy the land taken up by more than 200 of its neighbours.

The range of footprint values was large – from less than 0.5 to more than 40 ha per household. The high values were typically the result of large families with energy-inefficient homes taking one, or

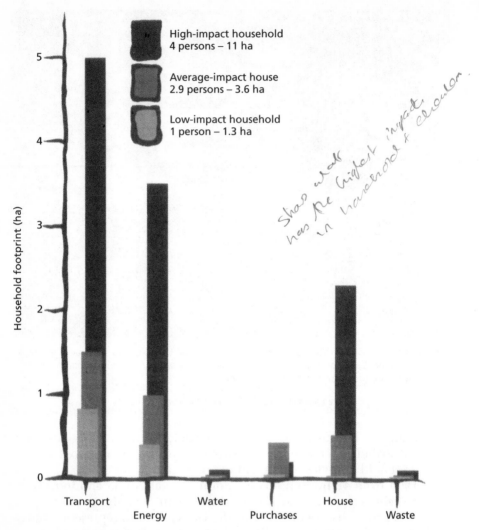

High-impact household
4 persons – 11 ha

Average-impact house
2.9 persons – 3.6 ha

Low-impact household
1 person – 1.3 ha

Note: For the average household, n = 42. Footprints expressed in local, rather than global, average bioproductive space

Figure 11.3 *Household footprints*

more, long-haul holidays abroad, coupled with one-off 'high impact' purchases (such as hardwood furniture, the impacts of which should probably have been accounted for over a longer period of time to reflect durability).

Figure 11.3 shows the comparative footprints of one large- and one small-impact household, alongside the footprint of the average household. Sample households are subdivided into the different categories measured by EcoCal. Transport generally ranks as the highest impact (average 1.53 ha), closely followed by direct energy use (average 0.99 ha); waste and water consistently score the lowest.

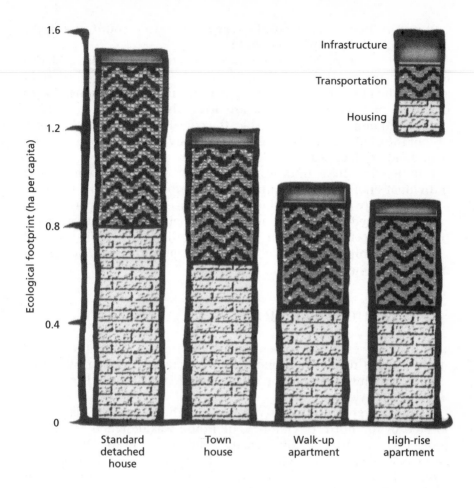

Source: Walker 1995[3]

Figure 11.4 *Ecological footprint by type of house*

As noted earlier, the figures for the latter two categories in particular are now believed to be artificially low. Recent improvements to the methodology treat waste and water more completely. Thus, if the study were reported with the more up-to-date conversion factors presented in Chapter 5, the results for waste and water in particular would be higher than those shown in Figure 11.3.

The findings are comparable with other work on the urban density of households undertaken by Walker in Canada,[2] where a restricted range of impacts (transport, energy and land use footprints) were calculated for five dwelling types: results ranged from 0.9 to 1.50 ha per capita depending on the size of property (see Figure 11.4).

The household footprint for a townhouse (the nearest equivalent to a typical UK house) is given in Walker's report as 2.71. When the other impacts measured by EcoCal – purchasing, water use, waste and so on (but not in the Canadian study) – are taken into account, the figure rises to around 3.5 ha per household.

It therefore seems likely that EcoCal is capturing many of the significant and controllable environmental consequences of household actions. The most obvious omission is in the area of purchasing, due to practical limits on questionnaire size. Inevitably, this leads to simplifications and omissions. For example, the consumption of takeaway and restaurant food was treated rather generously whilst the use of many household products was excluded altogether.

Guided by these findings, any public campaign to minimize individual environmental impact would probably wish to focus its resources firstly on household transport choices, then energy use. Even with the limited information on shopping habits, it seems that education about specific purchasing decisions would also yield benefits. Of course, consumption data may vary from region to region, necessitating different priorities.

THE SOLAR HOUSE – A CASE STUDY

The authors were eager to benchmark the findings from the EcoCal study using a regular household that had taken steps to live more sustainably whilst maintaining what most Westerners would consider a 'normal' lifestyle.

An ideal opportunity presented itself with the Oxford Solar House located in the north of Oxford. The house was designed as a living project to test the feasibility of using solar energy in the UK. It is the home of an Oxford academic,[3] and her family, for whom the house was built with the assistance of the UK Department of Trade and Industry, EA Technology and others.

The house was designed to consume the minimum amount of energy while providing a high quality living space. By most standards the solar house would be considered a luxury dwelling. It has all modern conveniences (washing machine, dishwasher, microwave, computer and security system for example), is set on three floors with four bedrooms and a total living space of around 250 m².

The house uses solar energy in three ways: photovoltaics (PV) generate electricity, there is a solar water heating system and the house is designed to benefit from passive solar heating, even in the winter. The passive solar heating occurs either radiantly, as the sun enters through windows and heats the thermal mass of the house, or convectively as warm air is taken in from a sun-space through floor- and ceiling-level vents.

Gas-fired appliances are used for cooking and, in winter, for evening heating. At ground level, a wood-burning stove is the main source of heat. Triple-glazed windows are used throughout. The fixed household lighting requirements have been met using low-energy

Table 11.2 *The Ecological Footprint for a Particular Lifestyle – Food only*

Categories	Amount per year (kg)	Fossil energy (m²)	Arable land (m²)	Pasture land (m²)	Sea (m²)
Fruit, vegetables	48	24	27		
Bread	36	72	85		
Rice, cereals, noodles	48	48	175		
Beans	48	48	563		
Milk, yogurt	36	36		717	
Cheese, butter	36	234		7171	
Eggs (50 g each)	144	936	92		
Meat					
Pork	12	96	262		
Poultry	12	96	153		
Beef (grain fed)	12	96	700		
Beef (pasture fed)	12	96		3636	
Fish	12	120			6621
Juice and wine	12	5	12		
Sugar	12	19	25		
Oil and fat					
Solid	12	47	65		
Liquid (l)	12	37	52		
Tea and coffee	12	90	212		
Eating out (complete meals)	12	24	58	273	
Total food		**2125**	**2480**	**11,798**	**6621**

fluorescent and halogen bulbs. The 'open' design of the house allows the maximum use to be made of natural daylight.

The occupants also make an effort to live a more environmentally sustainable lifestyle. They seek to reduce or recycle their waste, try to avoid air-freighted food products and, perhaps most significantly, run a small electric car, charged from the PV system. The house is not totally self-sufficient in electricity although it sometimes produces a surplus. Electricity is bought and sold via a metering system, drawing power when necessary from the national grid.

Limiting their analysis to the same set of questions and categories of impact as in the original EcoCal study (and using the same basic assumptions), the authors calculated the footprint of the Solar House to be 1.26 ha, which is equivalent to the lower scores obtained in the wider study. The analysis is considered to be a fair representation of the impact of the house, with the possible exception of the house and garden category where the standard EcoCal assumptions about the energy embodied in the building are probably an underestimate due to the additional energy required to produce the PV roof.

CALCULATING A MORE DETAILED LIFESTYLE FOOTPRINT

It is also possible to go beyond the basic questions asked within EcoCal and, where data permit, calculate a fuller personal lifestyle footprint. Table 11.2 shows an extract from a spreadsheet designed by Wackernagel and his colleagues to perform such an analysis. The spreadsheet poses more than 50 questions in the categories of food, housing, services, goods, transportation and waste. The conversion factors are expressed in world average productive space in square metres. The calculations are further calibrated to ensure that the average consumption pattern accurately reflects the more comprehensive national data analysis (as set out in Chapter 7).

For those interested in estimating their own household impacts, both EcoCal and the household spreadsheet described here are available on the Internet. A simplified 13-question on-line personal footprint calculator is also available.[4] Have a go at measuring your own ecological footprint – you may be surprised!

NOTES

1   Going for Green is Britain's biggest environmental awareness campaign. It is funded by both the Department of the Environment, Transport and the Regions and the public sector. It promotes the Green Code, a five point guide to small, individual actions which every household can take to help reduce damage to our environment. EcoCal is a registered trademark of Going for Green

2   Unpublished Masters thesis entitled 'The influence of dwelling type and residential density on the appropriated carrying capacity of Canadian households', Walker, 1995, School of Community and Regional Planning, University of British Columbia, Vancouver, BC

3   Dr Susan Roaf from the Planning Department at Oxford Brookes University, who kindly completed an EcoCal questionnaire for the authors

4   These resources are accessible from the web site http://www.ecologicalfootprint.com

Chapter 12

Next Steps

This book set out to explore environmental sustainability from the perspective of ecological footprint analysis. Footprinting is certainly not the only way to indicate ecological impacts, but the authors hope that they have shown you why – in their view – it is an invaluable pedometer on the road to a more sustainable future.

Our journey has, quite literally, covered a lot of ground – from the personal to global, forests to oceans, exploring both rich and poor countries. The authors trust that one message comes through loud and clear – that human consumption is most likely exceeding that which nature can regenerate. In other words, we are in overshoot, with a footprint larger than the carrying capacity of our planet. We are neither living within nature's interest nor, for that matter, sharing what is available in an equitable manner.

Yet ours is not a doom and gloom message. By adding to the knowledge of the impact of our species on planetary ecosystems, we sincerely hope that ecological footprinting can help to bring society closer to understanding and relating to the natural world.

The authors are encouraged by the positive efforts of scientists, writers, artists and governments to understand the imperative of living within the means of nature. Despite having turned from hunter-gatherers to supermarket browsers, it seems that humanity has not lost the instinct to survive.

We are all partaking in one big experiment where the stakes are high and the territory uncharted. There have never been so many mouths to feed, brains to think or hands to toil. But neither has the world ever before seemed so small or been so aware of its possible futures.

In every corner of the world, and without necessarily knowing it, we have become global citizens. Each of us has a role to play. Together we can take big steps and create the world we want.

Let's dance.

A Primer on Thermodynamics

Ecological footprint analysis is consistent with the laws of thermodynamics. An understanding of the following basic principles can provide a useful background to practitioners of footprinting.

1 *The conservation of matter: mass is neither created nor destroyed.* It is that simple: nothing disappears. Yes, we recognize that we need to be a bit more precise. 'Conservation of matter' needs a slight modification due to Einstein's energy/mass equivalency: $E=mc^2$. This equivalency says that mass can disappear and become energy. But even with very little mass loss, huge amounts of energy are liberated (the Nagasaki and Hiroshima nuclear bombs transformed about 1 gram of mass into energy). Also we recognize that the Big Bang that created our universe 15 billion years ago may have been a brief moment when 'conservation of matter', even with Einstein's modification, had been superseded. Ever since, however, this law has ruled; and it's one you will not get a ticket for when breaking it, because one cannot break it, as mischievous as one wants to be (and if you can, you'll get a Nobel Prize for sure). For practical matters, we can ignore Big Bang physics and Einstein's friendly amendment. In fact, the basic law of conservation of matter is good enough science for flying people to the moon. This simple law, though, has practical and profound implications. Recognizing the constancy of mass tells us that all matter that is not reabsorbed by nature accumulates somewhere in some way or another. It helps us to remember that there is no place called 'away'. In other words, nature will not suddenly forget something and make things 'mysteriously' disappear. You can lose objects – but they cannot disappear from the planet.

2 *The first law of thermodynamics: energy is neither created nor destroyed.* In a closed system, the amount of energy is constant. For example, the earth can only maintain its constant temperature if it radiates heat as rapidly as it receives solar energy (light). Or put another

way, the pot on the stove can only get hot as fast as it receives energy from the gas flame (minus all the heat from the flame that does not make it to the pot and heats other parts of the kitchen). The same is true for a mechanical system. Without friction, a mechanical system continues to move at the same speed. With friction, some mechanical energy is transformed into the same amount of heat. The overall amount of energy is the same – even though some form of energy has changed into another form of energy.

3   *The second law of thermodynamics: everything runs down.* More formally, this principle, which is also known as the 'entropy law', says that in a closed system the quality of energy decreases. A more fancy way is to say that 'the system's entropy increases'. In popular language one would hear people talk about energy being wasted. But in more precise terms, energy is never lost. It is merely transformed into a lower quality energy with less capacity to do useful work. For example, when we use the brakes on the bicycle we slow down. The kinetic (or movement) energy of the bicycle then heats the brake pads. The heat in the brake pads, however, cannot be used anymore to accelerate the bicycle again – it is of lower quality.

These laws help us to understand how the biosphere works. The sun, with its high-quality energy beaming on our planet, powers the biosphere and keeps our economy running. Photosynthesis transforms lots of high-quality light energy into less high-quality biomass and waste heat. Animals, including people, consume the biomass and produce a lot of waste heat and a few high-quality products (for example, as we eat biomass we produce human energy and a bit of human flesh). In other words, all the high-quality light energy eventually becomes heat that is radiated into the universe.

To this combination of the first and second laws we can add the law of mass conservation. The same amount of stuff that we eat, drink and inhale will leave our body again. If it didn't we would gain weight very rapidly. The key, though, is that the quality of the energy and matter we receive is much higher than the quality of the energy and matter we give back (oxygen, quality food, clean water, sweat, urine, excrement and CO_2). It is the difference in quality between the energy and matter that enter and eventually leave our bodies that fuels our organisms.

What does this all mean for footprinting? On the one hand, it helps us to understand the driving forces behind natural and human made systems. But even more specifically, it allows us to establish biophysical accounts of people's, households', cities' or countries' metabolisms. Since all the matter and energy entering a system must eventually leave again, these flows can be tracked on balance sheets. This means that it becomes possible to understand, monitor and manage the material and energy flows on which these entities depend.

Conversion Tables

Energy	Data	Unit
1 Gigawatt hour (GWh) is equal to:	85.98	tonnes of oil equivalents
	3600	gigajoules
	1,000,000	kilowatt hours
	34,120	therms (European)
	3,412,000,000	British thermal units (Btu)
	8,598,452,278,590	calories
1 tonne of oil equivalent is equal to:	10,000,000	kilocalories
	396.8	therms (European)
	41.87	gigajoules
	11,630	KWh
	39,680,000	British thermal units (Btu)

Length	Data	Unit
1 kilometre (km) is equal to:	0.621	miles
	1094	yards
	1000	metres
1 metre (m) is equal to:	100	centimetres
	39.4	inches
1 mile is equal to:	1.609	kilometres
	1760	yards
	1609	metres
1 passenger-km	1 person travelling 1 km	
1 tonne-km	1 tonne travelling 1 km	

Weight	Data	Unit
1 tonne (t) is equal to:	1000	kilogrammes
	1,000,000	grammes
	0.984	long ton
	1.102	short ton
	2205	pounds (lb)

Source: *Digest of United Kingdom Energy Statitsics 1999*, The Stationery Office, London

Volume	Data	Unit
1 litre (l) is equal to:	0.22	Imperial gallon (UK gal)
	0.26	US gallons

Area	Data	Unit
1 hectare (ha) is equal to:	10,000	square metres
	2.47	acres
	107,639	square feet

The following prefixes are commonly used:

kilo (k)	=	1000	or 10^3
mega (M)	=	1,000,000	or 10^6
giga (G)	=	1,000,000,000	or 10^9

Glossary

Appropriated carrying capacity is another name for the ecological footprint. 'Appropriated' signifies captured, claimed or occupied. Ecological footprints remind us that we appropriate ecological capacity for food, fibres, energy, waste absorption etc. In industrial regions, a large part of these flows is imported.

Anthropogenic – produced by human activities.

Biological capacity refers to the total of the biologically productive areas. See also 'biologically productive areas'.

Biologically productive areas are those areas of a country with quantitatively significant plant and animal productivity. Biologically productive areas of a country comprise its biological capacity. Arable land is potentially the most productive area.

Calorific value – The energy content of a fuel measured as the heat released on complete combustion.

Carbon dioxide (CO_2) – A gas which is naturally emitted by living organisms as well as during the combustion of fossil fuels. The latter is problematic since it leads to increased concentrations in the atmosphere.

Ecological deficit of a country or region measures the amount by which its footprint exceeds the locally available ecological capacity.

Ecological footprint is the land and water area that is required to support indefinitely the material standard of living of a given human population, using prevailing technology.

Ecological remainder or remaining ecological capacity. Countries or regions with footprints smaller than their locally available ecological capacity are endowed with an ecological remainder – the difference between capacity and footprint. Today, in many cases, this remainder is occupied by the footprints of other regions or countries (through export production). See also 'ecological deficit'.

Embodied energy of a commodity is the energy used during its entire life cycle for manufacturing, transporting, using and disposing.

Fossil fuels – coal, natural gas and fuels derived from crude oil (for example, petrol and diesel).

Hectare – one hectare (ha) is 10,000 square metres (100 x 100 metres). One hectare is equivalent to 2.47 acres.

Locally available capacity is the part of the locally existing ecological capacity that is available for human use. The remaining part should be left untouched for preserving biological diversity. In this book, we calculate the available capacity by subtracting 12 per cent from the existing capacity, as suggested by the Brundtland Report.

Locally existing capacity refers to the total ecological production that is found within a country's territories. It is expressed in hectares, usually based on world average productivity.

Natural capital refers to the stock of natural assets that yield goods and services continuously. Main functions include resource production (such as fish, timber or cereals), waste assimilation (such as CO_2 absorption, sewage decomposition) and life support services (UV protection, biodiversity, water cleansing, climate stability).

Overshoot, according to William Catton, is 'growth beyond an area's carrying capacity, leading to crash'.

Photosynthesis is the biological process in chlorophyll-containing cells that convert sunlight, CO_2, water, and nutrients into plant matter (biomass). All food chains that support animal life – including our own – are based on this plant matter.

Productivity is measured in biological production per year and hectare. A typical indicator of biological productivity is the biomass accumulation of an ecosystem.

Waste factors (used in round-wood calculations) give the ratio of one cubic metre of round wood used per cubic metre (or tonne) of product.

Yield adjusted area refers to the biologically productive space expressed in world average productivity. It is calculated by multiplying the physically existing space by the yield factors.

Yield factor is the factor by which a country's ecosystems are more productive than the world average. A yield factor of 0.5 indicates that local productivity is only half of the global average.

Index

recio 2 post bk
so maybe it would be
ideal e read his
also

'Since Wackernagel and Rees completed their initial treatise on ecological footprinting in the mid-90s the term has come to embrace a range of conceptual frameworks – not all of which satisfied the intellectual rigour of the original idea. Now at last we have a publication which not only restores that level of rigour, it reinforces the concept and adduces to it a far wider range of data, investigative work and research which now underpins the originality and innovativeness of the original thesis'

Peter Jones,
Director External Affairs,
Biffa Waste Services

'Measuring progress towards sustainability is a complex but important process. The ecological footprinting approach is a promising step forward. This book leads the way'

Alexander de Roo MEP,
Vice Chairman of the Environment, Public Health and
Consumer Committee,
European Parliament

'This book sets out the most important compass that society can have if we are to navigate the future'

Ed Mayo,
Executive Director,
New Economics Foundation

'This book shows ecological footprinting to be a vital tool to help assess our real impact on the planet. It should be read by every policymaker'

Paul Kingsnorth,
Deputy Editor,
The Ecologist

'*Sharing Nature's Interest* is an essential book for the citizen who wants to live in such a way that his or her grandchildren will inherit a planet in reasonably good order. It combines important advice for individual action backed by a dazzling display of science'

Tim Beaumont, Lord Beaumont of Whitley,
Green Party Representative in the UK House of Lords

LIVERPOOL
JOHN MOORES UNIVERSITY
AVRIL ROBARTS LRC
TITHEBARN STREET
LIVERPOOL L2 2ER